T0285330

GARETH FARR

Gareth Farr has worked as an actor at the RSC, Young Vic, West End, Royal Court, West Yorkshire Playhouse and Sheffield Theatres, as well as numerous television roles on programmes including *Misfits*, *Skins* and *Vera*. He has always been a writer and was part of the Royal Court's new-writing scheme and Super-Group.

His first play *Britannia Waves the Rules* won a Judges' Award at the 2011 Bruntwood Prize for Playwriting and went on to full production at the Royal Exchange Theatre, Manchester, in 2014. It was then taken on tour and played at the Edinburgh Festival Fringe before being revived in 2015 for a further tour. It has also been produced in Sydney, Australia. Gareth's second play *The Quiet House* was produced by Birmingham Rep and Park Theatre, London, in 2016. His third play *Shandyland* was shortlisted for the 2022 George Devine Award, and was in rehearsal at Northern Stage about to receive a full production when it was sadly cancelled due to the Covid-19 pandemic.

Gareth has taken part in the prestigious Old Vic 12 scheme and the BBC Studio Writers Academy. He has numerous TV scripts in development and his fourth play is scheduled for production at Bristol Old Vic in 2024.

Other Titles in this Series

Mike Bartlett
THE 47TH
ALBION
BULL
GAME
AN INTERVENTION
KING CHARLES III
MIKE BARTLETT PLAYS: TWO
MRS DELGADO
SCANDALTOWN
SNOWFLAKE
VASSA *after* Gorky
WILD

Chris Bush
THE ASSASSINATION OF KATIE HOPKINS
THE CHANGING ROOM
FAUSTUS: THAT DAMNED WOMAN
HUNGRY
JANE EYRE *after* Brontë
THE LAST NOËL
ROCK/PAPER/SCISSORS
STANDING AT THE SKY'S EDGE
    with Richard Hawley
STEEL

Jez Butterworth
THE FERRYMAN
JERUSALEM
JEZ BUTTERWORTH PLAYS: ONE
JEZ BUTTERWORTH PLAYS: TWO
MOJO
THE NIGHT HERON
PARLOUR SONG
THE RIVER
THE WINTERLING

Caryl Churchill
BLUE HEART
CHURCHILL PLAYS: THREE
CHURCHILL PLAYS: FOUR
CHURCHILL PLAYS: FIVE
CHURCHILL: SHORTS
CLOUD NINE
DING DONG THE WICKED
A DREAM PLAY *after* Strindberg
DRUNK ENOUGH TO SAY I LOVE YOU?
ESCAPED ALONE
FAR AWAY
GLASS. KILL. BLUEBEARD'S FRIENDS.
    IMP.
HERE WE GO
HOTEL
ICECREAM
LIGHT SHINING IN BUCKINGHAMSHIRE
LOVE AND INFORMATION
MAD FOREST
A NUMBER
PIGS AND DOGS
SEVEN JEWISH CHILDREN
THE SKRIKER
THIS IS A CHAIR
THYESTES *after* Seneca
TRAPS
WHAT IF IF ONLY

Gareth Farr
BRITANNIA WAVES THE RULES
THE QUIET HOUSE

Natasha Gordon
NINE NIGHT

Lucy Kirkwood
BEAUTY AND THE BEAST
    with Katie Mitchell
BLOODY WIMMIN
THE CHILDREN
CHIMERICA
HEDDA *after* Ibsen
IT FELT EMPTY WHEN THE HEART
    WENT AT FIRST BUT IT IS
    ALRIGHT NOW
LUCY KIRKWOOD PLAYS: ONE
MOSQUITOES
NSFW
RAPTURE
TINDERBOX
THE WELKIN

Suzie Miller
PRIMA FACIE

Winsome Pinnock
LEAVE TAKING
ROCKETS AND BLUE LIGHTS
TAKEN
TITUBA

Stef Smith
ENOUGH
GIRL IN THE MACHINE
HUMAN ANIMALS
NORA : A DOLL'S HOUSE
REMOTE
SWALLOW

Jack Thorne
2ND MAY 1997
AFTER LIFE
BUNNY
BURYING YOUR BROTHER IN
    THE PAVEMENT
A CHRISTMAS CAROL *after* Dickens
THE END OF HISTORY…
HOPE
JACK THORNE PLAYS: ONE
JACK THORNE PLAYS: TWO
JUNKYARD
LET THE RIGHT ONE IN
    after John Ajvide Lindqvist
THE MOTIVE AND THE CUE
MYDIDAE
THE SOLID LIFE OF SUGAR WATER
STACY & FANNY AND FAGGOT
WHEN YOU CURE ME
WOYZECK *after* Büchner

debbie tucker green
BORN BAD
DEBBIE TUCKER GREEN PLAYS: ONE
DIRTY BUTTERFLY
EAR FOR EYE
HANG
NUT
A PROFOUNDLY AFFECTIONATE,
    PASSIONATE DEVOTION TO
    SOMEONE (– *NOUN*)
RANDOM
STONING MARY
TRADE & GENERATIONS
TRUTH AND RECONCILIATION

Phoebe Waller-Bridge
FLEABAG

Gareth Farr

BISCUITS FOR BREAKFAST

NICK HERN BOOKS

London

www.nickhernbooks.co.uk

A Nick Hern Book

Biscuits for Breakfast first published in Great Britain in 2023 as a paperback original by Nick Hern Books Limited, The Glasshouse, 49a Goldhawk Road, London W12 8QP

Cover image: photography by iStockphoto/vasantytf; design by Nick Warren at N9 Design

Designed and typeset by Nick Hern Books, London
Printed in Great Britain by Mimeo Ltd, Huntingdon, Cambridgeshire PE29 6XX

A CIP catalogue record for this book is available from the British Library

ISBN   978 1 83904 218 8

Woodland CARBON
www.woodlandcarbon.co.uk
NICK HERN BOOKS
Printed on Carbon Captured paper

Biscuits for Breakfast was first performed at Hampstead Theatre, London, on 5 May 2023. The cast was as follows:

PAUL	Ben Castle-Gibb
JOANNE	Boadicea Ricketts
DAD	Giles King
YOUNG PAUL	Rufus Flowers
Director	Tessa Walker
Designer	Cecilia Carey
Lighting	Matt Haskins
Sound	Holly Khan
Movement	Rebecca Wield

Acknowledgements

Thanks to Nick Bagnall, Dan Parr, Amber James, Lewis Peek, Jennifer Galt, Kuldip Singh-Barmi, Rebecca Wield, Jeanette Maggs, Boadicea Ricketts and Benn Castle-Gibb for all of their help in developing the play.

Thanks also to Arts Council England and Theatre Royal Plymouth for supporting the R&D. Thanks to Giles King, Rufus Flowers, Christian Aindow, AMATA and Falmouth University for all of their help with the recordings.

Special thanks to Rupert Cooper from Philleigh Way and to the real-life superhero Simon Fann from Truro Foodbank for their belief in our 'foodbank recipe cards' project.

Extra special thanks to Kristian Wall, Liam McLaughlin and all at Just Add Milk productions for the original commission of *Biscuits for Breakfast*. And to Roxana Silbert and Tessa Walker for believing in this play and for bringing it to Hampstead Theatre.

Huge thanks to everyone at Hampstead Theatre for making it happen.

Extra, extra special thanks to Tessa Walker for asking the right questions and pushing for the right answers and for being completely brilliant from start to finish. And finally, massive thanks to Gabby Vautier for always being there, no matter what.

G.F.

To my mum and dad
who told me stories
and encouraged me to dream big

Characters

PAUL
JOANNE

YOUNG PAUL, *recorded*
DAD, *recorded*

This text went to press before the end of rehearsals and so may differ slightly from the play as performed.

PAUL *and* JOANNE *stand looking at each other. The hissing static sound of a tape player is heard.*

YOUNG PAUL (*on tape*). Dad!

DAD (*on tape*). On here.

YOUNG PAUL (*on tape*). Found you, Dad.

DAD (*on tape*). You did.

YOUNG PAUL (*on tape*). Wanna help me?

DAD (*on tape*). Not now.

YOUNG PAUL (*on tape*). Please. Come on, Dad, need your help with my homework.

DAD (*on tape*). Where's your mum?

YOUNG PAUL (*on tape*). Dunno. At home somewhere.

DAD (*on tape*). Find her.

YOUNG PAUL (*on tape*). Found you. Found you, Dad. Need help with my homework.

DAD (*on tape*). Tired.

YOUNG PAUL (*on tape*). Tired. You haven't done anyfin'. Just sat here all day. Can't get tired from sittin' on a boat.

DAD (*on tape*). You can.

YOUNG PAUL (*on tape*). Please. Please, Dad, please.

DAD (*on tape*). Working tonight.

YOUNG PAUL (*on tape*). That's ages away. I need a story. Got to write a story. I wanna record one of yours and copy it.

DAD (*on tape*). Turn that thing off.

YOUNG PAUL (*on tape*). No.

DAD (*on tape*). I don't like it.

YOUNG PAUL (*on tape*). Yeah you do. You listen to them all the time. I've heard you listening to them on here.

DAD (*on tape*). If I tell a story, you do something for me.

YOUNG PAUL (*on tape*). Deal. What is it?

DAD (*on tape*). Too late. You already made the deal.

YOUNG PAUL (*on tape*). Not cooking.

DAD (*on tape*). You already made the deal.

YOUNG PAUL (*on tape*). Nooo!

DAD (*on tape*). I'll tell you a story while we cook and then we can eat it together.

YOUNG PAUL (*on tape*). Boring.

DAD (*on tape*). Not boring. Special.

YOUNG PAUL (*on tape*). Just food nothing special about that.

DAD (*on tape*). Food is so, special, Paul. It's in everything I do, see. I catch food, I sell food, I cook food. If you can do one of those things, you'll always be in work. People always need to eat, see? People will always need food. Cooking's the best one of them all. Calming. Safe. There's pride in it, y'know?

YOUNG PAUL (*on tape*). Yeah.

DAD (*on tape*). But, if you can cook properly, if you know flavour and taste and texture, people will pay you to do it. You learn how to cook well, if you get really good at it, you can get rich doing it, son. Imagine that. You can be rich, you can be better. You can be so much better than here.

YOUNG PAUL (*on tape*). I like it here.

DAD (*on tape*). You do now. One day you'll want more.

The tape stops.

...

Music. Like a pub. JOANNE *is stood drinking.* PAUL *walks over to her.*

PAUL. Alright?

JOANNE. Alright.

PAUL. Wanna beer?

JOANNE *looks at him. She leaves.*

...

One week later. Music. Like a night club. JOANNE *is stood drinking.* PAUL *walks over to her. The music is so loud we can't fully hear what they say.*

PAUL. Alright?

JOANNE. What?

PAUL. I said alright?

JOANNE. What?

PAUL. Are you alright?

JOANNE. Yeah. I'm fine. Why?

PAUL. What?

JOANNE. Why are you asking if I'm alright?

PAUL. I don't know. You're on your own.

JOANNE. Yeah.

PAUL. Wanna beer?

JOANNE. I've got a beer.

PAUL. Do you want another one?

JOANNE. Do I want two beers?

PAUL. Yeah.

JOANNE. No.

JOANNE *looks at him. She leaves.*

...

*One week later. Music. Like a gig. JOANNE is stood drinking.
PAUL walks over to her. The music is so loud we can't fully
hear what they say.*

PAUL. Alright?

JOANNE. Oh, my God!

PAUL. I said, alright?

JOANNE. I know.

PAUL. Are you alright?

JOANNE. Yeah. I'm fine. Why?

PAUL. What?

JOANNE. Why are you asking if I'm alright week after week?

PAUL. I don't know.

    I.

    I was just. Do you want a beer? You've finished that one.

JOANNE. No.

PAUL. Oh. Why not?

    JOANNE looks at him. She leaves.

...

Moments later. Outside.

PAUL. Alright?

JOANNE. Oh my God!

PAUL. What?

JOANNE. What is that? Alright. Is that the best you can do?

PAUL. No.

JOANNE. Go on then, do better.

PAUL. Sorry, you're just...

JOANNE. What? I am just, what?

PAUL. You're on your own.

JOANNE. Yeah. I am. And?

PAUL. Nothing. It's cool. Coming out on your own. I think that's cool.

JOANNE. Yeah? And now I'm going home on my own.

PAUL. I'm not a prick.

JOANNE. I'll get you a medal.

PAUL. I'm not a wanker.

JOANNE. Not a prick?

PAUL. No.

JOANNE. Not a wanker?

PAUL. No. I'm normal.

JOANNE. Normal?

PAUL. Yeah.

JOANNE. Wow.

PAUL. I'm Paul.

JOANNE. Goodnight, Normal Paul.

PAUL. I'm decent. I'm a good lad.

JOANNE. Leave a girl alone then when she's asking you to leave her alone.

PAUL. Yeah. Of course.

PAUL steps back. He leaves. JOANNE watches him go.

···

One week later. Music plays – like a gig. PAUL is stood drinking, watching the band. JOANNE enters. They notice each other. PAUL keeps his distance. They watch the band. They keep noticing each other. JOANNE smiles. She walks over to him.

JOANNE. Alright?

PAUL. Alright.

JOANNE. Wanna beer?

...

Two weeks later.

PAUL. Alright?

JOANNE. –

PAUL. Sorry. Hello. Hi. Welcome.

JOANNE. Hello, Normal Paul.

PAUL. What's your... I don't even know your –

JOANNE. Joanne.

PAUL. Cool. I never got the
        chance to...   JOANNE. No. Yeah. Joanne.

PAUL. Joanne. Got it. You look nice.

JOANNE. Easy.

PAUL. You do. The hair and –

JOANNE. Can I come in then or are we having a barbecue?

PAUL. Sorry.

   They enter his flat.

JOANNE. What is it?

PAUL. What's what?

JOANNE. Dinner.

PAUL. Oh, fish pie.

JOANNE. Right.

PAUL. What?

JOANNE. Nothing. Smells good.

PAUL. Ta. From Newlyn.

JOANNE. What is?

PAUL. The fish. Landed and smoked this morning.

JOANNE. Is that supposed to be good then?

PAUL. Yeah.

JOANNE. I get mine from SPAR.

PAUL. You should get it from Newlyn. Cheaper. Fresher.

JOANNE. Posher.

PAUL. No. Not –

JOANNE. Got egg in it?

PAUL. Egg?

JOANNE. Yeah, boiled egg. In the pie.

PAUL. No.

JOANNE. I like boiled egg in mine.

PAUL. In fish pie?

JOANNE. Yeah. What's wrong with that?

PAUL. Nothing. Just not what I –

JOANNE. This your flat?

PAUL. No.

JOANNE. No? What're you doing in it then?

PAUL. It's my brother's. He's letting me stay here for a bit.
     He's travelling.

JOANNE. Nice. Where?

PAUL. Dunno. Australia. Somewhere like that.

JOANNE. Somewhere like Australia?

PAUL. Yeah.

JOANNE. New Zealand then?

PAUL. Er. Dunno.

JOANNE. Joke. That was a joke. How long for?

PAUL. Oh. He's coming back next year. Visa runs out.

JOANNE. What happens then?

PAUL. Get my own spot.

JOANNE. Where?

PAUL. Dunno.

JOANNE. Newlyn?

PAUL. Maybe.

   Beat.

JOANNE. I'm not staying.

PAUL. What? You've only just – I've made a fish pie.

JOANNE. The night. I'm not getting into bed with you so –

PAUL. No. I know. I wasn't thinking –

JOANNE. I'm just saying. I'm just being straight.

PAUL. Fair. Fair.

JOANNE. In case you were wondering.

PAUL. I wasn't. Well, I'm not now.

JOANNE. I'm just. Y'know?

PAUL. What? No. What?

JOANNE. For the grub.

PAUL. Sure.

JOANNE. You said you were good. So, I thought fuck it.

PAUL. I am good.

JOANNE. Where is it then?

PAUL. It's not ready yet.

JOANNE. Right.

PAUL. I am, though.

JOANNE. What?

PAUL. Good. I am good at cooking.

JOANNE. So you keep saying.

Silence. It's awkward. She looks around the flat. She notices something.

What's that meant to be?

PAUL. What?

JOANNE. That boat. What's it meant to be?

PAUL. Not meant to be anything. Just a boat.

JOANNE. It's a toy boat.

PAUL. It's not a toy.

JOANNE. Yeah it is.

PAUL. It's not.

JOANNE. What is it then?

PAUL. Dunno. It's just a…

JOANNE. Toy.

PAUL. It's nothing. It's an ornament… whatever.

JOANNE. An ornament?

PAUL. Yeah.

JOANNE. You've got an ornament of a toy boat?

PAUL. Yeah. No. Just a boat.

JOANNE. Why?

PAUL. Just have.

JOANNE. Twenty-five-year-old lads don't have ornaments, they have PlayStations.

PAUL. It's just a boat. What's the problem?

JOANNE. No problem. Don't get your pants twisted.

PAUL. I'm not.

Beat.

JOANNE. Put it in the bath with you?

PAUL. No.

JOANNE. Is it Playmobil?

PAUL. No.

JOANNE. Are you sure?

PAUL. It's a trawler.

JOANNE. Right.

PAUL. For fishing.

JOANNE. Right.

PAUL. My dad gave it to me.

JOANNE. Right. Cool. It's cool. I'm just –

PAUL. What?

JOANNE. Nothing. Messing about.

Beat. Tension. A step too far.

PAUL. I'll get a PlayStation for next time.

JOANNE. Next time?

PAUL. Y'know what I mean.

JOANNE. Let's just see how the fish pie is first. If I spend half the night gipping, then there won't be no next time, brother.

PAUL. Do you want a drink?

JOANNE. Got a beer?

PAUL. Yeah.

He goes to get her one. JOANNE *stays, anxious. She can't settle.*

PAUL *returns and hands her a beer.*

JOANNE. Is it from Newlyn?

PAUL. No. ASDA.

JOANNE. Posh… It's a bit small.

PAUL. The beer?

JOANNE. The flat.

PAUL. Is it?

JOANNE. Yeah.

PAUL. Where do you live, Buckingham Palace?

JOANNE. –

PAUL. What?

JOANNE *smiles. It's the first time.*

My dad used to work there.

JOANNE. At Buckingham Palace? Bollocks.

PAUL. Newlyn.

JOANNE. Oh. Right. I was gonna say.

PAUL. Newlyn.

JOANNE. Alright, you can stop saying Newlyn.

PAUL. His boat's still moored there, so…

JOANNE. Fishing was it?

PAUL. Yeah.

JOANNE. Not any more then?

PAUL. No.

JOANNE. Don't blame him. Tough gig, I reckon.

PAUL. EU fucked him. Fucked 'em all.

JOANNE. I don't do politics, mate.

PAUL. You would if you were a fisherman.

JOANNE. You wouldn't if you grew up in care.

A step too far. Neither of them knows where to go from here.

You ever done it?

PAUL. What?

JOANNE. Fishing?

PAUL. No. Not proper.

JOANNE. Why not?

PAUL. Dunno.

JOANNE. You should. Fucking, sea air in your pants. It'd sort you right out.

PAUL. Don't fancy it.

JOANNE. Give a man a fish and he'll eat for a day, teach a man to fish and he'll sit in his boat and drink beer all his life.

PAUL. That's right.

JOANNE. What's he do now then, your dad?

PAUL. Nothing.

JOANNE. Easy life, is it?

A timer sounds.

PAUL. It's ready.

JOANNE. Cool.

PAUL. I'll get the food.

PAUL exits. JOANNE wrestles her anxiety. She looks at the boat. She looks at it closely. She touches it. PAUL re-enters. We don't see food. They don't mime. We just know they have served and eaten.

It's hot.

JOANNE. Smells good.

PAUL. How is it?

JOANNE. I've not had any yet.

They eat.

Nice.

PAUL. Yeah?

JOANNE. Yeah.

PAUL. Good.

They eat.

JOANNE. Better than the SPAR.

PAUL. I'll take that. Put it on the cover of my book.

JOANNE. Put an egg in next time.

PAUL. Next time?

They smile. They eat. The mood settles.

JOANNE. What's all this about then?

PAUL. What?

JOANNE. Cooking? Bit weird. Grab hold of someone in a club and cook her fish pie. It's a new one on me.

PAUL. I didn't grab hold of you.

JOANNE. No.

PAUL. You were on your own.

JOANNE. So?

PAUL. Nothing.

JOANNE. I like going out on my own.

PAUL. It's cool. I'm training.

JOANNE. Yeah? What, at pulling girls? You need to do better.

PAUL. You're here, aren't you?

JOANNE. Fresh.

PAUL. Cooking. I'm training to be a chef.

JOANNE. Fair. College, is it?

PAUL. No. Hotel.

JOANNE. Oh yeah? Which one?

PAUL. Regent.

Something shifts. JOANNE *stares at him.*

JOANNE. Oh yeah?

PAUL. Yeah.

JOANNE. How's that?

PAUL. Good. Yeah. Okay. My hands get fucked a bit, but other
    than that –

JOANNE. Why?

PAUL. Washing up. Chemical cleaning. Soft skin and hot pans.

JOANNE. Knives.

PAUL. Sometimes.

JOANNE. Big knives.

PAUL. Not really. I watch them… the chefs. They're brilliant.
    Serious with it… with the food, y'know? Pride in it. I do the
    sauces.

JOANNE. Sauces?

PAUL. Sauces and soups. Not the big stuff yet. I cook here
    though. Try out dishes. Keeps me level. Take it round to my
    mum's. Neighbours. Let them have some. Shit like that.

JOANNE. Expensive.

PAUL. I borrow ingredients from work.

JOANNE. Borrow?

PAUL. To practise with. They let me take some stuff.

JOANNE. Right.

PAUL. Only if I can't get it myself. Only little bits. Herbs and shit. I get the other stuff from mates. Not mates, people I know. Farmers and fishermen. Leftovers.

JOANNE. You following me?

PAUL. What? No.

JOANNE. The Regent Hotel?

PAUL. I saw you once.

JOANNE. It's cool.

PAUL. I only saw you once.

JOANNE. It's cool. You're following me.

PAUL. I'm not.

JOANNE. It's cool. It's level as fuck. I'll eat up and be off.

PAUL. I saw you once and then I saw you out –

JOANNE. Three times.

PAUL. Yeah. But –

JOANNE. I'm easy about it, mate. Let's eat. Is it poisoned?

PAUL. No.

JOANNE. Rohypnol? Cos that shit doesn't work on me –

PAUL. Give over. I'm not following you. I saw you once in the fucking break room and then I saw you in the club on your own and I fancied you a bit, so I said hello. Nothing more than that. Honest. I'm not going to poison you with fish pie. Why would I want to do that?

JOANNE. I don't know. Psycho.

PAUL. Calm down. Go home if you want.

JOANNE. I might.

PAUL. You can't, the doors are locked, and the walls are soundproofed.

JOANNE. Prick.

PAUL. I've got a cage in the cellar, gonna put you in it and feed you five-star fish pie every day.

JOANNE. You don't joke about things like that on a first date.

PAUL. A date, is it?

JOANNE. I didn't mean that.

PAUL. Yes you did! Yes, you did!

JOANNE. No.

PAUL. It's a date?! I never said this was a date! You said it was a date. I'm just feeding a –

JOANNE. What?

PAUL. Nothing.

JOANNE. Feeding a what?

PAUL. Nothing.

JOANNE. Loner?

PAUL. Friend. I was going to say friend.

JOANNE. I don't know you.

PAUL. I know. That's why I didn't say it.

JOANNE. So –

PAUL. I get it. It's not a date. I'll keep my distance. It's just the grub.

JOANNE. Yeah.

PAUL. Which is excellent, so.

JOANNE. I never said that.

PAUL. You didn't need to. Eaten it all. Speaks for itself.

Silence. Things settle. They look at each other.

JOANNE. Fancy me a bit do ya?

PAUL. It's just for the grub, I get it.

Beat. Something shifts.

JOANNE. Gonna do seconds then, or what?

They smile.

...

Two weeks later. PAUL *is teaching* JOANNE *to cook.*

JOANNE. What's that?

PAUL. You know what that is. Kids know what that is.

JOANNE. Looks like a messed-up onion.

PAUL. Shallot.

JOANNE. Posh.

PAUL. Let me show you how to use a knife.

JOANNE. I know how to chop an onion.

PAUL. It's not an onion it's a shallot. Chop it like this.

PAUL *shows her how to chop a shallot.*

JOANNE. Smooth.

PAUL. Yeah?

JOANNE. Looks like you're showing off.

PAUL. Maybe I am.

JOANNE. Bit fit as it goes.

PAUL. Now, you do it the same.

JOANNE *does.*

Sharp knife, be careful of your fingers.

JOANNE. You don't need to worry about me, mate.

PAUL. Pan hot?

JOANNE. Yes, chef! Hot to trot.

PAUL. Get it in there then and move it about a bit.

JOANNE. Kinky.

PAUL. –

JOANNE. What next?

PAUL. Garlic.

JOANNE. Oooh. No kissing tonight.

PAUL. Ginger.

JOANNE. The stuff you use!

PAUL. It's only ginger.

JOANNE. Looks like summat they brought back from the moon.

PAUL. Keep stirring.

JOANNE. I am.

PAUL. Keep it moving. You leave it still and it'll spoil, it'll burn.

JOANNE. I'll spoil you in a minute. Getting all serious.

PAUL. It'll taste like shit if it burns.

JOANNE. Relax, I'm smashing this.

PAUL. How's it looking?

JOANNE. Dunno. A bit brown, I guess. Burned? Maybe a bit /
burned.

PAUL. Fuck's sake!

JOANNE. Calm down, it's only burned a little bit. Pick that bit
out, easy.

PAUL. Right, now we put the paste in. Mix that up.

JOANNE. JESUS!!

PAUL. What?

JOANNE. Burning my eyes.

PAUL. Give over.

JOANNE. Is it meant to smell like that?

PAUL. Yes.

JOANNE. Smells like dog shit and lighter fluid. Like when you pour lighter fluid on dog shit and burn it. You ever done that?

PAUL. No. Of course not.

JOANNE. Smells like this. It smells exactly like –

PAUL. Fish sauce.

JOANNE. Eurgh!!! Oh my GOD!! That's worse, mate. That is disgusting. Not eating this! Fucking stinks.

PAUL. Coconut milk. Sugar.

JOANNE. –

PAUL. And some salt and pepper. Turn the heat down. Put the chicken back in and let it simmer.

JOANNE. Yes, chef.

PAUL. Better?

JOANNE. Suppose.

PAUL. Yeah?

JOANNE. Yeah. Smells alright now. Smells good.

PAUL. Leave it alone for five minutes. It's gonna taste amazing.

JOANNE *looks at* PAUL.

What?

JOANNE. I don't know anyone who can cook like this.

PAUL. You probably do it's not that hard.

JOANNE. Everyone I know eats Pot Noodle with sandwiches dunked in.

PAUL. Nothing wrong with that.

JOANNE. Yes there is. There's a lot wrong with that.

PAUL. Depends what flavour Pot Noodle you're having. That Sticky Rib one is amazing.

JOANNE. What do you do now?

PAUL. Wait. Clean down. Watch it closely.

JOANNE. That all?

PAUL. Yeah. Why? What you –

   JOANNE *kisses him.*

   Right. Yeah. Cool. We could do that.

JOANNE. What?

PAUL. Nothing. Just, not what I normally do.

JOANNE. You might be normal, Paul, but I'm not.

PAUL. No. I get that.

   JOANNE *kisses him again. It lasts longer.* PAUL *breaks away.*

JOANNE. What? If you're not into it, then just fucking say, don't be all –

PAUL. Rice.

JOANNE. Rice? What about it?

PAUL. It's ready.

JOANNE. Oh. So?

PAUL. It might burn.

   Beat. JOANNE *senses his anxiety and plays with it.*

JOANNE. Leave it. I dare you.

   She kisses him again. It doesn't last long before PAUL *breaks away.*

PAUL. Really. It might burn.

JOANNE kisses him again, he backs away.

I'm stressing about it.

JOANNE. Serve it up then. I'd had enough anyway. Don't wanna get too excited, do we?

We don't see it, they don't mime, but the food is served.

What's that now?

PAUL. Coriander.

JOANNE. Standard.

They sit and eat.

PAUL. What do you reckon?

JOANNE. –

PAUL. What? What?

JOANNE stands up and paces about.

JOANNE. Shut the fuck up!

PAUL. What?

JOANNE. I mean… that is unreal… that is… shut up, stop talking to me now. Let me concentrate. Leave me alone. Let me eat.

He smiles. They eat.

...

Two weeks later.

PAUL *and* JOANNE *look at two bowls.*

JOANNE. The fuck is that?

PAUL. Soup.

JOANNE. Is it? What sort of soup?

PAUL. Beetroot.

JOANNE. Beetroot soup? Who the fuck eats that?

PAUL. It's good.

JOANNE. Looks like blood.

PAUL. Well it's not.

JOANNE. Looks like something from a hospital or an abattoir or a –

PAUL. It's beetroot soup. With star anise.

JOANNE. What?!

PAUL. I dunno. It's a herb, or a spice. I dunno. Makes it taste good.

JOANNE. Posh.

PAUL. A bit, yeah. Taste it.

    JOANNE *tastes*.

JOANNE. –

PAUL. What?

JOANNE. –

    JOANNE *tastes again. She smiles*.

PAUL. Good, right?

JOANNE. Yeah. I thought it was gonna taste rotten, but it doesn't.

PAUL. I'll take that.

JOANNE. I've never… I've never had anything like that before.

PAUL. Proper.

JOANNE. Did you nick it?

PAUL. What?

JOANNE. The star thing?

PAUL. No. It's like a quid from ASDA.

JOANNE. Posh.

PAUL. I'm gonna take it to the head chef at The Regent. Gonna try and get it on the menu.

JOANNE. Yeah?

PAUL. In autumn. Seasonal.

JOANNE. Right. Cool.

PAUL. And then, when I've made a name for myself, I'll have it on the front cover of my book. Signature dish.

JOANNE. What book?

PAUL. Gonna have a cookbook. Gonna write one.

JOANNE. Are ya?

PAUL. Yeah. All my recipes. I've learned loads. Collected them. Got hundreds.

JOANNE. Sounds good.

PAUL. Got to dream, right? Got to push for something.

JOANNE. Dunno. Have you?

PAUL. Yeah. Course.

JOANNE. If you say so.

PAUL. What else is there around here? Dreams and sea. That's all there is. Dreams and sea and rain. So, fuck it. I'm gonna have a cookbook. Other people have got one so –

JOANNE. Yeah, famous people.

PAUL. Not always.

JOANNE. You gonna be on the telly?

PAUL. No. Just gonna graft and get something real. Something that's mine. Something better than this.

JOANNE. Better?

PAUL. Yeah.

JOANNE. Why better?

PAUL. Because washing pans and making soup all day is just
the start. Can't stay there forever.

JOANNE. What, and a cookbook's gonna change that, is it?

PAUL. Change it for me. Cookbook first, restaurant after.
Local food, y'know? Cornish. Sell loads and make
something that lasts. Bust out, move up, make something
good somewhere else.

JOANNE. Right. See ya then.

PAUL. What?

JOANNE. Nothing, mate. It's cool. Get one. Get a book and
fuck off.

PAUL. I will. I'm gonna.

JOANNE. Get a cookbook with a bowl of blood soup on the
front. See what it does for ya.

PAUL. S'up with you?

JOANNE. Nothing wrong with me. You go ahead, mate. Get
a book.

PAUL. Where's this come from?

JOANNE. What?

PAUL. Getting shitty. Pissing on people's dreams.

JOANNE. Soz. Just a joke, don't cry.

PAUL. It's just ambition, that's all. What are you into then,
other than taking the piss?

JOANNE. Nothing. Just that.

PAUL. What are you gonna leave behind when it's all just rain
and shadow?

JOANNE. Rain and shadow, what's that mean, rain and
shadow?

PAUL. Just… what you gonna leave behind to prove that you were here?

JOANNE. Don't need to leave nothing behind, mate. What's the point?

PAUL. Loads of point.

JOANNE. Nope.

PAUL. You must want to do something.

JOANNE. I do something.

PAUL. What, cleaning hotel rooms is what you live for, is it?

JOANNE. Yeah.

PAUL. Dirty bedding is the stuff of dreams for you, is it?

JOANNE. Proper.

PAUL. No way.

JOANNE. All the way.

PAUL. All your life?

JOANNE. Yeah. Why not? I love it.

PAUL. Bullshit.

JOANNE. Is it?

PAUL. Yeah, must be.

JOANNE. Can't all be superstars, Paul. World wouldn't work if everyone sat around chasing dreams. Some of us have got to clean up after you. Someone's got to do the jobs that you're all too good for.

PAUL. I wasn't saying that. You could do anything you want to, that's all.

JOANNE. I am doing what I want to. Why do I want to do anything else if I'm happy?

PAUL. Be better.

JOANNE. Better?

PAUL. Do something better.

JOANNE. Be better?

PAUL. Yeah, y'know?

JOANNE. You keep saying that. Better than what?!

PAUL. Better, just better.

JOANNE. Better than happy. What is that?

PAUL. You know what I mean.

JOANNE. Do I? Do I know what you mean, Paul? Good at
    telling me stuff about myself, aren't ya? Think you know me?
    I'm cool. I'm not running from nothing, brother. I'm just here.
    Don't need to be better.

PAUL. I was just –

JOANNE. You don't need to fix nothing here, mate.

PAUL. Not fixing.

JOANNE. Known me five minutes and trying to make me
    better.

PAUL. Why you getting arsey for?

JOANNE. Not arsey, mate. Not arsey. Just reacting.

PAUL. You give it out.

JOANNE. Yeah. All the time.

PAUL. Comes back your way though –

JOANNE. What is this? Trying to teach me something? Some
    fat fucking lesson about hopes and dreams, is it?

PAUL. No.

JOANNE. Good.

PAUL. Right.

JOANNE. Right.

PAUL. Why are you here?

JOANNE. I'm not. I'm going. It was all a bad dream.

PAUL. You give it out.

JOANNE. You said that, brother. You keep saying it but not meaning anything.

PAUL. But you can't take it.

JOANNE. I don't need to take it. Don't need to be anything for you.

PAUL. You need to be polite.

JOANNE. Do I?

PAUL. Yeah.

JOANNE. Why?

PAUL. I dunno. Because it's decent.

JOANNE. Why do I need to be decent?

PAUL. Because people are.

JOANNE. I'm not.

PAUL. Clearly.

JOANNE. Step back, now. Too judgey, mate. It's all got stressy and weird.

PAUL. This is nonsense. I don't even know why you are getting all –

JOANNE. Soup's gone cold, Paul. Tastes shit cold. Thought you should know. Put that in your book. Bye.

JOANNE *leaves the space.* PAUL *stands still. He is uncomfortable and doesn't know what to do with his hands. Eventually* PAUL *starts to move. He starts to cook.*

...

One week later. JOANNE *and* PAUL *stand on his doorstep.*

PAUL. What's that?

JOANNE. What's it look like?

PAUL. Beer.

JOANNE. Ten points to Hufflepuff.

PAUL. Ta.

JOANNE. Got it for you.

PAUL. Ta.

JOANNE. To say sorry for being all aggy.

PAUL. Cheers.

JOANNE. You can have a cookbook. I think it would be good if you did. Sorry for pissing on it.

PAUL. S'alright.

JOANNE. Drink it then.

PAUL. I don't really –

JOANNE. S'from Newlyn.

PAUL. Right.

JOANNE. Went all the way down there on the bus, see what all the fuss is about. Saw that and thought you could curl up with it. Marry it.

PAUL. Funny.

JOANNE. I know. Drink it then. One won't kill you.

He does.

How is it?

PAUL. Good. Bit warm but good.

PAUL *hands her the beer.*

I'm sorry too.

JOANNE *takes the beer and drinks.*

JOANNE. Gonna invite me in then?

They go inside.

Tidy.

PAUL. Yeah.

JOANNE. Very tidy.

PAUL. Yeah.

JOANNE. You heard the news then?

PAUL. Yeah.

JOANNE. Taken it well I see.

PAUL. It's bollocks.

JOANNE. Fair.

PAUL. It's bullshit.

JOANNE. Yep.

PAUL. It is though.

JOANNE. I'm not disagreeing with you.

PAUL. It's bullshit. It's a joke.

JOANNE. It'll be fine.

PAUL. Will it?

JOANNE. Yeah.

PAUL. When though?

JOANNE. Dunno. Just got to relax.

PAUL. Relax?

JOANNE. Yeah. No point having a stress attack about it.

PAUL. Are you for real?

JOANNE. Real deal. I'm easy breezy me, mate.

PAUL. You live there.

JOANNE. I know. That is a problem.

PAUL. Can they do that? Can they just kick you out like that?

JOANNE. Hotel's closed. No customers, no job, no living quarters.

PAUL. How long you got?

JOANNE. Week, ten days tops.

PAUL. Fuckers.

JOANNE. They've gone bust, they're not bad people. They can't catch cash when there's no cash about, that's all. Not just The Regent, others are closing too.

PAUL. What you gonna do?

JOANNE. Dunno.

PAUL. Where you gonna live?

JOANNE. Thought I might move in here.

> PAUL *stops moving. They look at each other.*

You alright with that?

PAUL. Serious?

JOANNE. It's a bit pokey but the food's good.

PAUL. –

JOANNE. Got nowhere else to go, mate.

PAUL. No.

JOANNE. So…

PAUL. Right.

JOANNE. Just for a bit. Sofa and that, nothing heavy. Nothing –

PAUL. It's not my place.

JOANNE. So?

PAUL. Jimmy's coming back. He'll be back in January.

JOANNE. Till January then. Gonna make me beg or what?

PAUL. Got to keep up the rent to the council. If I don't –

JOANNE. Yeah. We will. Get a job. Get another job.

PAUL. Doing what?

JOANNE. Shifts going at the garlic bread factory. Got a trial
    there tomorrow. Reckon I could get you in there too if
    you want.

PAUL. No ta.

JOANNE. Why not? S'cash.

PAUL. I just… I dunno… I don't want to.

JOANNE. Cover the rent, n'that.

PAUL. I'll wait.

JOANNE. Wait? What for?

PAUL. Something better.

JOANNE. Better? Stressing a minute ago. I'll do it. I don't care.
    I'll make smelly bread and cover the rent. Council won't
    know shit. Just until you're back chopping again.

PAUL. –

JOANNE. See how it goes.

PAUL. –

JOANNE. Please? Fuck's sake.

PAUL. Course. Yeah. No worries.

JOANNE. Cool. Thanks.

PAUL. They'll be open again soon. Hotels do this all the time.

JOANNE. Yeah.

PAUL. Have you back. Have us both back.

JOANNE. Totally. I'll be out of your hair double soon.

Pause.

Want fish and chips? Got to have fish and chips on moving-
in day.

PAUL. No ta.

JOANNE. My treat. Salt and vinegar and soggy paper. The best.

PAUL. I'm alright.

JOANNE. I'll get large. You'll want some when you smell 'em.

PAUL. I won't.

Nobody moves.

JOANNE. Got a spare key?

PAUL. No.

JOANNE. I'll just knock, shall I?

PAUL. Need to get one cut.

PAUL gives her his key.

JOANNE. You chased me, y'know? Called it on.

PAUL. What? I know.

JOANNE. So, don't get all weird.

PAUL. I'm not. It's cool.

JOANNE. Is it?

PAUL. Yeah.

JOANNE. Good. Back in a bit.

*She goes. PAUL stands still. Eventually he moves and pulls
out a small box. He takes out a tape and puts it into a tape
player. The static sound of a tape recorder is heard. During
the recording PAUL starts to cook.*

DAD (*on tape*). Love you, Paul.

YOUNG PAUL (*on tape*). Dad!

DAD (*on tape*). I do. Love cooking with you. Keeps me level.

PAUL *rewinds and plays it again.*

DAD (*on tape*). Love you, Paul.

YOUNG PAUL (*on tape*). Dad!

PAUL *rewinds and plays it again.*

DAD (*on tape*). Love you, Paul.

YOUNG PAUL (*on tape*). Dad!

DAD (*on tape*). I do. Love cooking with you. Keeps me level.

YOUNG PAUL (*on tape*). I know, Dad. Same.

DAD (*on tape*). Will you make me a promise, Paul?

YOUNG PAUL (*on tape*). What is it?

DAD (*on tape*). Dream big. Be better.

YOUNG PAUL (*on tape*). Don't know what that means.

DAD (*on tape*). Just work hard. Be better than here.

YOUNG PAUL (*on tape*). You drunk?

DAD (*on tape*). No!!

YOUNG PAUL (*on tape*). Can we just cook then?

DAD (*on tape*). Sure. You alright to chop this?

YOUNG PAUL (*on tape*). Yeah.

DAD (*on tape*). Sharp knives, Paul.

YOUNG PAUL (*on tape*). Yeah.

DAD (*on tape*). Watch your fingers.

YOUNG PAUL (*on tape*). I will.

DAD (*on tape*). Don't get cut.

YOUNG PAUL (*on tape*). I won't.

DAD (*on tape*). Don't get burned.

YOUNG PAUL (*on tape*). I won't.

DAD (*on tape*). Good lad...

 Beat.

 Got you something.

YOUNG PAUL (*on tape*). Yeah? What?

DAD (*on tape*). Present.

YOUNG PAUL (*on tape*). Yeah? Why?

DAD (*on tape*). Just saw it. Made me think of you.

YOUNG PAUL (*on tape*). What is it?

DAD (*on tape*). Open it and find out.

 YOUNG PAUL *opens the present.*

YOUNG PAUL (*on tape*). Boat.

DAD (*on tape*). Not just any boat.

YOUNG PAUL (*on tape*). Did you get Jimmy a boat?

DAD (*on tape*). No.

YOUNG PAUL (*on tape*). What did Jimmy get?

DAD (*on tape*). Nothing.

YOUNG PAUL (*on tape*). What? I got a boat and Jimmy didn't get anyfin'?

DAD (*on tape*). Not just any boat. She's a trawler.

YOUNG PAUL (*on tape*). Is she fast?

DAD (*on tape*). No.

YOUNG PAUL (*on tape*). Oh.

DAD (*on tape*). Do you know what a trawler is?

YOUNG PAUL (*on tape*). Fishing. Like this one. Like our boat.

DAD (*on tape*). She's a working boat. A boat for life. Brings people food, Paul. We bring people food. Special, that. An outrigger like this looks after you. When a storm comes and it's all rain and shadow, a boat like this will keep you safe, she will carry you home.

YOUNG PAUL (*on tape*). Yeah?

DAD (*on tape*). Yeah. She will keep the storm away.

YOUNG PAUL (*on tape*). I want a racer. I want the fastest boat there is. I don't care about the storm.

DAD (*on tape*). You will. One day a storm will come, and you'll need a boat like her.

The tape stops.

...

PAUL *steps onto the deck of the boat. He helps* JOANNE *on. She is less steady on her feet than he is.*

JOANNE. This it then?

PAUL. Her.

JOANNE. What?

PAUL. Boats are always she or her. She's a bit battered now but I do my best to look after her.

JOANNE. Sleep on here?

PAUL. Sometimes. Not really. Bit baltic in winter. Bit baltic in summer.

JOANNE. Got a stove. You cook on here?

PAUL. Used to. Not any more. It needs gas.

JOANNE. Moves about a bit.

PAUL. Yeah.

JOANNE. Take it out? Catch some grub?

PAUL. Her.

JOANNE. Sorry. Serious about that, aren't ya?

PAUL. It's just a thing.

JOANNE. Come on then, fire her up. Let's hear her roar.

PAUL. No diesel.

JOANNE. Oh right. So, it just sits here, does it? Bobbing up
and down?

PAUL. She… and yeah.

JOANNE. Put some music on.

PAUL. What?

JOANNE. Tapes, all those tapes. Retro.

PAUL. That's not… No power. No diesel, to charge the battery.

JOANNE. Right. What're we doing, on here then?

PAUL. Dunno, Just showing you.

JOANNE. Right. Well, *she's* lovely.

PAUL. Yeah.

JOANNE. Cold.

PAUL. Yeah.

JOANNE. Really, really cold.

PAUL. Yeah, I know.

JOANNE. No diesel to warm the battery or whatever.

PAUL. No. I just said that.

JOANNE. Gonna, have to keep warm somehow. Gonna have to
do whatever we can to keep warm, aren't we?

PAUL. Oh. Yeah.

They kiss. They laugh. They kiss.

...

Two weeks later. JOANNE *enters after her first shift at the garlic bread factory.* PAUL *is stood still.*

JOANNE. Alright?

PAUL. Yeah.

JOANNE. Sure?

PAUL. Yeah. Why?

JOANNE. Dunno. Just look spaced.

PAUL. Fine. Just y'know.

JOANNE. What?

PAUL. Bored.

JOANNE. Bored? Plenty to do out there, mate. Plenty to keep you busy if you want it.

PAUL. How was it?

JOANNE. Alright. You should get on it. Laugh-a-minute.

PAUL. D'you have to do?

JOANNE. Big tub of butter mixed with garlic, like a bucket, I think it was actually a bucket, like from B&Q. Spatula, like from Wilko's and then bread, like from SPAR. Slap the butter on the spatula, slap the spatula all over the bread, pass it on to the grated-cheese guy, who passes it onto the salt dude, get another one, repeat. Eight hours.

PAUL. Jesus.

JOANNE. S'alright. Had the radio on. Done worse.

PAUL. Have you?

JOANNE. Yeah, definitely. Oh, guess what I did on the way home?

PAUL. What?

JOANNE. I went shopping.

PAUL. What did you get?

JOANNE. Wait for it… Ta, dah!

    JOANNE *reveals a jar of jam from her bag*.

PAUL. Jam.

JOANNE. And…

    JOANNE *reveals and loaf of bread*.

PAUL. Bread.

JOANNE. It's a classic.

PAUL. Anything else?

JOANNE. Yeah.

    JOANNE *produces two Pot Noodles*.

    Sticky Rib. Your favourite.

PAUL. No eggs? No flour?

JOANNE. Flour? No.

PAUL. Cool.

JOANNE. You okay?

PAUL. Yeah.

JOANNE. S'up?

PAUL. Nowt. Tired.

JOANNE. Tired? You haven't done anything. Can't be tired of sitting here all day.

PAUL. I'm fine. Let's eat. Bread and jam and Pot Noodle.

JOANNE. You go shopping on four and a half quid, see what you get.

PAUL. It's fine.

JOANNE. I suppose you'd come back with some double rare golden radish that only grows when a rainbow shines.

PAUL. No.

JOANNE. Cheer up then.

PAUL. I am. It's great.

JOANNE. Butter?

PAUL. What?

JOANNE. We got any butter?

PAUL. Yeah. Not much.

JOANNE. I'll see if I can 'borrow' some from work tomorrow.

PAUL. See if they have any flour and eggs as well.

JOANNE. They have butter, garlic, cheap cheese, a million bottles of table salt and B&Q buckets. That's it.

PAUL. Get some buckets and salt.

JOANNE. What for?

PAUL. Can use 'em.

JOANNE. Right. Okay, then, I'll look forward to that little mystery. Tonight, however, it's my turn to rustle up the grub. Tonight, I cook for you. Tonight, we have Pot Noodle with bread dunked in and then jam sandwich for pud, and you are going to fucking love it. Tonight, we do it my way.

PAUL. Cool.

JOANNE. We can do this, mate. We can. As long as we pay the council we're cool, you said.

PAUL. It's cool.

JOANNE. It's cool then. Fucking garlic bread factory is going to save us, mate. Might just stink for a few weeks that's all.

PAUL. I can deal with that.

JOANNE. Good. Cos it gets everywhere, under your skin, in your nose. Feet. It makes your feet stink apparently. It's all you can smell they reckon. Gave us a talk about it.

PAUL. Few weeks, you reckon?

JOANNE. It's going to be okay. I'm at the wheel, mate. Gonna steer us to safety. It's going to be okay.

PAUL. Cool.

JOANNE. Cool. I'll boil the kettle.

JOANNE leaves.

PAUL stands alone. A memory floods into his mind. The hissing static of the tape can be heard. YOUNG PAUL *and* DAD *are cooking.*

DAD (*on tape*). Pan hot?

YOUNG PAUL (*on tape*). Yeah.

DAD (*on tape*). Put them in then.

The sound of cooking fills the space.

Keep them moving.

YOUNG PAUL (*on tape*). I will.

DAD (*on tape*). You leave them still and they'll spoil.

YOUNG PAUL (*on tape*). I won't.

DAD (*on tape*). Leave anything still for too long and it will spoil, Paul. You know that?

YOUNG PAUL (*on tape*). Yeah.

DAD (*on tape*). Got to keep things moving.

YOUNG PAUL (*on tape*). I will. Tell me a story, Dad.

DAD (*on tape*). What kind of story?

YOUNG PAUL (*on tape*). Scary story, tell me a scary one.

DAD (*on tape*). Poach the fish and pass me the bottle and I'll tell you a story about buried treasure.

JOANNE returns with two Pot Noodles.

PAUL. Wanna hear a story?

JOANNE. Is it funny? Needs to be funny.

PAUL. No. It's sad.

JOANNE. No thanks. Don't need no sad stories.

PAUL. There's this amazing place out west called Jenny's Prayer.

JOANNE. Oh, right we're doing it anyway. Fair enough.

PAUL. We're going there tomorrow.

JOANNE. Are we? Why?

PAUL. Treasure.

JOANNE. Talking about?

PAUL. Going to find buried treasure.

JOANNE *becomes interested.*

JOANNE. Okay. Treasure sounds good. Why's it called Jenny's whatever?

PAUL. Jenny's Prayer.

JOANNE. Yeah, why's it called that?

PAUL *sings.*

PAUL. Dear old Jenny Swinson,
   Fell in love with a smuggler's son,
   Caught him heavy, caught him true,
   Caught and fought when her father knew.
   Jenny lost him, Jenny cried, Jenny waited, and Jenny died.
   Jenny prayed for her smuggler's son,
   God love Jenny Swinson.

JOANNE. Don't give up your day job. Oh, wait a minute, you haven't got one.

Beat.

Joke. 'Twas a joke, mate. Too soon. Carry on.

PAUL. Jenny Swinson fell in love with a smuggler's son.

JOANNE. Yeah, I got that bit.

PAUL. They'd meet on the beach in the middle of the night. He had a voice on him apparently. That's how they'd meet each other. He'd sing to her in the dark so she could find him. Jenny's dad found out. Fought to keep them apart.

JOANNE. Sounds like a nice chap.

PAUL. Old-man Swinson had history with Old-man Smuggler. So, he wasn't having his daughter with Smuggler's son. Fought to keep them apart.

JOANNE. What sort of history?

PAUL. Old-lady Swinson. Jenny's mum.

JOANNE. What about her?

PAUL. Used to go at it with the Old Smuggler.

JOANNE. Whaaaaat? Good girl, you get yours, love. This is getting good now. Carry on.

PAUL. That's why Old-man Swinson didn't want Jenny with Smuggler's son.

JOANNE. Why? What's she got to do with –

The penny drops.

Nooooooo!! She was the old smuggler's daughter?

PAUL. Old-man Swinson knew about it but brought her up as his own, but when she started playing about with Smuggler's son –

JOANNE. Her brother.

PAUL. He had to stop it, didn't he?

JOANNE. Filth! I'm guessing he didn't just sit them down and explain it calmly, did he?

PAUL. No.

JOANNE. Gonna be about blood and thunder now, this story, isn't it?

PAUL. He locked Jenny in their house...

JOANNE. Right. Rational.

PAUL....and he went down to the beach where she would meet Smuggler's son. Listened out for his singing. Followed the sound in the dark.

JOANNE. Right.

PAUL. Found a big fucking rock and stoved his head in.

JOANNE. Whhhaattt?

PAUL. Told you it's a sad one.

JOANNE. Blokes. Always want to break stuff, always want to smash stuff up.

PAUL. Different times.

JOANNE. You reckon? What happened to Jenny?

PAUL. Her dad let her out and gave her a lantern, told her to go and find him. She ran down to the beach and found Smuggler's son all dead and bleeding. She picked him up and carried him to the water's edge. Tide took him. She watched him drift out and go under. Sent Jenny mad. Story goes that she never went home. She never left that beach from that moment on. She stayed out there singing and praying for him to come back. Beach is called Jenny's Prayer and they call the sound out there, Smuggler's song. Reckon you can hear him some nights. Old folk reckon they've seen her lantern.

JOANNE. And we're going there tomorrow?

PAUL. We're gonna try. Hard to get down there now, the path's all gone. But if we can get down there, if we can get to the beach, there's treasure.

JOANNE. What kind of treasure?

PAUL. Beautiful, incredible buried treasure, that nobody knows about.

...

PAUL *and* JOANNE *are at Jenny's Prayer.* PAUL *is holding a B&Q bucket.* JOANNE *is holding a bottle of table salt. They both look at the ground.*

PAUL. See that?

JOANNE. No. What?

PAUL. That hole.

JOANNE. Yeah.

PAUL. Salt it.

JOANNE. Why? Thought we were digging for treasure?

PAUL. We are. Salt it.

> JOANNE *pours salt on the hole.*

> That's enough. Wait. Wait.

JOANNE. I'm waiting.

> *Suddenly the salt moves.* JOANNE *jumps, genuinely terrified.*

> THE FUCK WAS THAT?!

PAUL. Watch.

JOANNE. The fuck is down there, mate?

PAUL. Dinner.

JOANNE. Joking!

PAUL. Pick it up.

JOANNE. Piss off. No chance. Looks like a monster.

PAUL. Go on.

JOANNE. I'm not touching that, looks like something from *Alien.*

PAUL. I dare you.

JOANNE. Will it bite?

PAUL. No, it won't bite, you dickhead. Pull it out.

JOANNE *goes to grab whatever is poking out of the sand and pulls away, freaked out. She goes again and pulls away. She takes a deep breath.*

Quick, then before it goes.

JOANNE *screams and lunges at the thing in the sand.* PAUL *laughs. She continues to scream as she holds up a razor clam as if it's something from another planet.*

JOANNE. What is it?! What is it?! What have I caught?

PAUL. Calm down.

PAUL *takes the clam.*

Good one.

JOANNE. What is it?

PAUL. Razor clam.

JOANNE. For eating?

PAUL. Boil it up with some onions and garlic and cream. Be good if we had white wine and saffron but we don't.

JOANNE. No. Not sure we've got the other stuff to be honest.

PAUL. No.

JOANNE. We might have an onion. Onion and razor fish. You'll do something with it. That the treasure then?

PAUL. That and other stuff. The freshest foraging in the country on this beach, beautiful food just sat on the ground, and nobody knows about it. Microclimate attracts all sorts of rareness.

JOANNE. Where d'you learn all this?

PAUL. Dad. Used to come here with him.

JOANNE. Nice. Let's get digging then.

PAUL. We need about ten more.

JOANNE. Easy beans, I'm on it.

> JOANNE *continues to look.* PAUL *stands and listens to the waves.*

S'up with you? Work to do, brother.

PAUL. Good being outside. Space.

JOANNE. Space?

PAUL. Space and sky and sea.

JOANNE. The big three.

PAUL. Can you hear that?

JOANNE. What?

PAUL. Waves.

JOANNE. Waves?

PAUL. Like the sea's breathing.

JOANNE. Yeah?

PAUL. That noise has been here for millions of years. That sound is older than mountains. The dinosaurs heard that noise. Can you believe that? You are listening to what the dinosaurs heard. And when we are all gone and it's just empty, just nothing, the emptiness will hear it too. That sound will still be here. Forever. Massive, that.

JOANNE. Makes me need a piss.

PAUL. Jesus.

JOANNE. What? It's all the water. It affects me.

PAUL. Well I can't help with that.

JOANNE. I need a wee now.

PAUL. Okay.

JOANNE. No toilet.

PAUL. Nope.

JOANNE. Got a bucket.

PAUL. You're not using my clam bucket to piss in.

JOANNE. Why not?

PAUL. Because it's for the food.

JOANNE. Only got one. Take it out, I'll do the deed and rinse it in the sea after.

PAUL. Or?

JOANNE. What?

PAUL. Get in.

JOANNE. Get in what?

PAUL. The sea.

JOANNE. Piss off.

PAUL. Why not?

JOANNE. I'm not getting in there to do a piss.

PAUL. Everyone does it.

JOANNE. I'm not everyone, mate. Freezing.

PAUL. It's July.

JOANNE. So?

PAUL. So, it won't be cold.

JOANNE. Joking, mate. Look at it. It's practically solid.

PAUL. Get in.

JOANNE. What about jelly monsters? What if I get bitten?

PAUL. Jellyfish don't bite, they sting.

JOANNE. That then.

PAUL. It's nothing. Like a stinging nettle. You'll be fine.

JOANNE. Stinging nettle on my lady-bits is not fine. I had one on my foot once, it went black.

PAUL. I'll keep an eye out. If I see a jellyfish near you, I'll grab it.

JOANNE. It's your fault making me listen to the stupid waves.

PAUL. Get in. Quick piss. Get out again. Feel better immediately. Carry on looking for dinner.

JOANNE. What about crabs and lobsters and things with claws?

PAUL. If you find a lobster, grab it. I'll have the fucker in a pot, and we'll be smiling for days.

JOANNE. Funny.

PAUL. You doing it then?

JOANNE. No.

PAUL. Scared?

JOANNE. No. I'll just find some rocks, get behind them and do it.

PAUL. Walkers will see you.

JOANNE. So.

PAUL. Walkers with binoculars and smartphones that zoom in.

JOANNE. Why are you saying that, now?

PAUL. Sea's the best place for it. Everyone knows it.

JOANNE. Coastal folk are weird as fuck.

PAUL. Unless you're scared.

JOANNE. No. Course not. I'll get in there. No worries.

PAUL. Go on them. I'll hold your clothes.

Pause. JOANNE *stares at the sea.*

JOANNE. If I drown, I want you to stay on this beach forever, singing and moaning.

PAUL. Deal.

JOANNE. Until they rename it, Normal-Paul's-idiotic-idea-of-a-stupid-fucking-joke-and-now-everyone-fucking-hates-him beach.

PAUL. Get in!

JOANNE. Ah, bollocks.

JOANNE runs into the sea. She screams. PAUL laughs.

You think this is funny?

PAUL. Yeah.

JOANNE. Freezing. I can't do it now.

PAUL. You have to focus. You have to force it out against the pressure of the water. Physics.

JOANNE. The stuff you know. S'pose the dinosaurs did this too, did they?

PAUL. Just do it so we can get on with the clams.

JOANNE. I can't.

PAUL. You can. Concentrate.

JOANNE. Shut up giving me instructions then and I will.

Pause.

I'm doing it. It's coming out.

PAUL. Congratulations.

JOANNE wades out of the sea.

JOANNE. Right come here, you little fucker.

She chases him. She catches him. They kiss. The sound of the sea grows and grows. It becomes the hissing sound of static.

...

Two weeks later. PAUL sits still. JOANNE enters.

JOANNE. Wanna go out?

PAUL. What? Where?

JOANNE. Pub. Pub then club.

PAUL. Serious?

JOANNE. Yeah, why not?

PAUL. Bit skint as it goes. Got no cash.

JOANNE. S'on me. Garlic bread paid today. Did two double shifts and four nights this month so we are in the gravy.

PAUL. How much?

JOANNE. Got enough for the rent. Don't worry, I've done my sums. Covered it for another month and now I want some hooch. Come on, I'll buy you a beer. Put a straw in it, get you pissed quicker.

PAUL. Don't want to get pissed.

JOANNE. I do.

PAUL. Do you reckon they'll open again soon?

JOANNE. Who?

PAUL. Regent.

JOANNE. Dunno. Not heard. Doubt it.

PAUL. Went knocking today. Asked around for work. Nothing going anywhere. Can't even get work at the carvery.

JOANNE. Keep looking.

PAUL. Saw half the chefs from The Regent, all making ends meet somewhere. Good chefs working in pubs. No jobs left.

JOANNE. Something will shake soon.

PAUL. Stressing me out.

JOANNE. Is it?

PAUL. Yeah.

JOANNE. Let's go out then, blow the cobwebs away and all that.

PAUL. I'm alright.

JOANNE. Are you?

PAUL. Yeah.

JOANNE. A little bit of hooch will make you feel great though.

PAUL. I fancy staying in.

JOANNE. Honest?

PAUL. Too many people.

JOANNE. What? Where?

PAUL. Out there.

JOANNE. Yeah. There are people out there.

PAUL. I'm not into it.

JOANNE. Not into people?

PAUL. No.

JOANNE. Right. Cool.

Silence. Stillness.

I'll be in The Seaview for starters, just half-dead locals in there so it should be safe if you fancied joining me.

PAUL. No ta.

JOANNE. After that it's anyone's guess. But if you turn on your Joanne radar, I'm sure you'll find me.

PAUL. No ta.

JOANNE. Okay. Bye then.

PAUL. Yeah.

JOANNE *exits.* PAUL *stands still. He doesn't know what to do with his hands.*

A memory consumes him. The hissing static of the tape can be heard.

DAD (*on tape*). Will you make me a promise, Paul?

YOUNG PAUL (*on tape*). What is it?

DAD (*on tape*). Dream big. Be better.

YOUNG PAUL (*on tape*). Don't know what that means.

DAD (*on tape*). Just work hard. Be better than here.

...

One week later. PAUL *is sat. He has been sat like this for some time.* JOANNE *enters.*

JOANNE. Morning all.

PAUL. –

JOANNE. Morning.

PAUL. Morning.

JOANNE. You good?

PAUL. Yeah. Just a bit…

JOANNE. What?

PAUL. Dunno. Tired.

JOANNE. Tired, again? You've only just got up, haven't you? Been asleep for nine hours. Can't be tired.

PAUL. Hungry.

JOANNE. Hungry now, is it?

PAUL. Yeah. Starving. Didn't have tea last night.

JOANNE. Right. I see. What have we got for breakfast then?

PAUL. Nothing.

JOANNE. Nothing? Bollocks. There's bound to be something.

PAUL. Got any money left?

JOANNE. Dunno.

PAUL. Got any money for food left?

JOANNE. Dunno. No. I don't think so.

PAUL. Drank it all?

JOANNE. Got biscuits. I'll have them.

PAUL. Biscuits.

JOANNE. Yeah. Want one?

PAUL. No.

JOANNE. Can't say you're hungry and then turn down food.

PAUL. Biscuits.

JOANNE. Yeah.

PAUL. What are we going to have for dinner?

JOANNE. I don't know. We haven't had breakfast yet, let's worry about dinner at dinner time. We'll find something.

PAUL. Will we? Where?

JOANNE. Well you ain't gonna find food sat in a chair, staring at the walls, brother. Might have to get your shoes on at least.

PAUL. And go where?

JOANNE. Dunno. Foraging? Fishing?

PAUL. No diesel. Boat won't go without diesel.

JOANNE. Newlyn then. Get down there, rub up a couple of salty old sea dogs, see if they can throw you a bone with a big fish wrapped around it.

PAUL. No.

JOANNE. Why not? They know you. Tell 'em you'll pay them back. Be alright.

PAUL. Begging.

JOANNE. No. Not begging. It's called getting a little bit of help. Folk love to help if they can.

PAUL. You go then. You go down the harbour, see what you get.

JOANNE. I fucking will, big man. Soon as I've finished making the country's finest garlic bread, I'll be straight down there. I'll get a fish for tea. I love a challenge, me.

PAUL. Is this a game?

JOANNE. A game? Dunno. Can be if / you want.

PAUL. Is this a big fucking joke!?

JOANNE. Easy now.

PAUL. What are we going to eat tomorrow?

JOANNE. I haven't even sorted today yet.

PAUL. Cracking the funnies.

JOANNE. Yeah. And?

PAUL. Stop it.

JOANNE. Why? Why stop it? I'm just trying to keep it friendly.

PAUL. Is that right?

JOANNE. Yeah, cos if I listen to much more of your misery chat, I'm going to hurt myself. We'll be fine.

PAUL. Will we?

JOANNE. If we crack on and don't crumble, yeah.

Beat. PAUL *takes a deep breath. He is holding on.*

PAUL. Sorry.

JOANNE. It's cool.

PAUL. Hungry.

JOANNE. Have a biscuit.

Beat.

What about your mum?

PAUL. What about her?

JOANNE. Can't she lend us summat?

PAUL. Like what?

JOANNE. Dunno. Bit of cash.

PAUL. No.

JOANNE. Grub then. Pasta. Some veg. I don't need much.

PAUL. No.

JOANNE. Just until I get paid. Garlic bread has been slow this month, taken on a load more people so my shifts are down. I'll do nights. More cash on nights. No fucker wants to do nights. Pay her back double next month.

PAUL. No.

JOANNE. Okay. Well at least we tried, at least we gave it a really massive try.

PAUL. It's about sustainability.

JOANNE. Sustainability? What's that then? Sounds like the *Six O'Clock News* in here.

PAUL. If we have biscuits for breakfast then it fills a hole for an hour but what then? What happens after the hour? More biscuits if we have them. The biscuits run out and what then? Eat Marmite from the jar. What then? What happens tomorrow or the day after? All the time that we have no food just increases the amount of time since we had any. Stressing me out.

JOANNE. I can tell.

PAUL. And I can't cook jokes.

JOANNE. No. No. I get it. Just need to adapt.

PAUL. Biscuits for breakfast ain't adapting. It's fucking up. It's failing hard.

JOANNE. At least I'm trying. At least I'm up off my arse and bringing in some wedge. At least I do a shift. Biggest shift you've done recently has been inside your own stressed head.

PAUL. I don't want to make garlic bread for a living.

JOANNE. Neither do I, prick. Nobody *wants* to make garlic bread for a living. Not one person on the planet *wants* to do that. But they do it. They do it because they have to. Because there is no other choice.

PAUL. You seem to enjoy it.

JOANNE. Because I'm tough as fuck and don't take shit seriously. Think it's nice down there? Think people are all fucking sitcom happy to work there? They're not. They're miserable as fuck and they let you know it. Hard. People are made out of stone down there, mate. Fucking rock solid with sharp edges. Rock solid and racist. I'm not bouncing down the road, mate. I take the shifts, I take the looks and the comments and nudges and the wankers spitting near me, because there's no choice. Because we need to pay the council and you don't want to. So, I do. So, I do.

PAUL. People spit at you?

JOANNE. Near me. I said near me. He did it once.

PAUL. Still.

JOANNE. Don't get fizzy about it, mate. That's nothing. Done it all my life. Alien round here me, mate. Got three heads. Got laser beams for eyes. Got funny-coloured skin.

PAUL. Do something.

JOANNE. Do what?

PAUL. I dunno. Tell someone?

JOANNE. Who? Boss? Because he's the one that spat.

PAUL. Fucking launch at 'em.

JOANNE. What then?

PAUL. Can't handle this? Can't breathe now. Can't fucking break out of this now.

JOANNE. You wanna try sixteen years in foster care, that'd toughen you right up.

PAUL. Don't know what to do now.

JOANNE. Live with it and crack on.

PAUL. This is broken. This is so fucking broken, now. Like I'm in a net and I can't breathe.

JOANNE. Right.

PAUL. Turning and getting tighter. Whichever way I turn it just gets worse and tighter.

JOANNE. Stop turning then. Settle it down a bit and swim on.

PAUL. Can't.

JOANNE. Have to.

PAUL. Can't.

JOANNE. You will.

PAUL. I won't. I can't. I can't breathe.

JOANNE. Stop making it all about you.

PAUL. What?

JOANNE. Just settle it down a bit and crack on.

PAUL. People spit at you and you're all right about it.

JOANNE. Getting grumpy won't stop the spitting. Just makes you grumpy and you've still got spit on you.

PAUL. This is fucked.

JOANNE. Is it? Feels very normal to me.

PAUL. Like I'm in a net.

JOANNE. Right well, this has been lovely, but I've got to go.

PAUL. Where?

JOANNE. Work. Double shift. Cracking on.

Pause. JOANNE *looks at* PAUL, *he's got nothing.*

No?

Bye then.

JOANNE *steps to leave.*

PAUL. Reckon you could get me a job then?

JOANNE. Thought you didn't want to.

PAUL. I don't. I don't. Can't just sit here though, can I?

JOANNE. I can try. They've just taken a load on, but I can try. Come with. Let them see the whites of your eyes.

PAUL. Like snakes and ladders around here.

JOANNE. Is it?

PAUL. Like snakes and ladders without the ladders.

JOANNE. Get changed, have a wash, let's go.

PAUL. Need to look smart, then?

JOANNE. No. Not really. Just… I don't know. Sharpen up a bit. Asking for a job, aren't you? Got to sharpen up and give it your best.

PAUL. Right.

PAUL *leaves the space.* JOANNE *watches him go. Tension. Pressure building.*

...

Five days later.

JOANNE. If you could eat anything right now, what would it be?

PAUL. Don't.

JOANNE. Go on. It's only a game. You can have anything.

PAUL. Fucking want to make me cry or something?

JOANNE. No. Trying to entertain you, mate. Trying to bring the joy. Distract you, whatever.

PAUL *thinks.*

Come on.

PAUL. Steak.

JOANNE. Yeah? Go on.

PAUL. Fourteen-day-air-dried, grass-fed, twenty-four-ounce, prime sirloin.

JOANNE. Detailed. I like it. Carry on.

PAUL. Olive oil on a high heat. Meat goes in, gently. Got to lay it in gently so it lies even. Salt. Black pepper. Four minutes. Turn it. Lay it back in the pan. Four minutes. Thirty seconds before taking it out, rub it with butter, both sides. Lay it back in the pan, let the butter do its work. Out of the pan and onto a chopping board, gently. Rest for two minutes so all the tension from the heat relaxes down. Sharp knife, a really good knife that glides through the meat, probably a Laguiole or an Umogi. Slice it nice. Mustard, the tiniest bit of Dijon mustard. In. Taste. Got to wait and taste. Chew. Swallow.

Beat.

That. That's what I'd have.

JOANNE. Blimey.

PAUL *is still imagining the steak.* JOANNE *waits for him to ask her. He doesn't.*

JOANNE. Angel Delight...
would be mine. In case you   PAUL. Right, sorry, yeah.
were –   What? Angel Delight?
                                                  Really?

JOANNE. Butterscotch.

PAUL. Don't.

JOANNE. It's amazing.

PAUL. Tastes like shit. Looks like shit. Like eating plastic-flavoured shit that's been whipped into a mousse.

JOANNE. Was living with a family for a while. They made it. I'd never had it before. Family food. What families eat. Like eating safety.

PAUL. Right. Yeah. Go on.

> JOANNE *remembers*.

JOANNE. Nah. Nothing to tell. It tasted good. It tasted really
good for a little while. I'd have that.

...

*Two weeks later. JOANNE enters. She is holding a plastic bag.
She takes out a banana and places on the table. She looks at it.
She cuts it in half and eats her half. She is hungry, the taste and
feeling of eating is intense. She looks at the other half of the
banana.*

JOANNE. Paul. Paul.

> PAUL *enters*.

> Someone left a banana on the table at work, so I took it.

PAUL. Right.

JOANNE. Saved you half.

PAUL. Thanks.

JOANNE. I was gonna eat it all, but I didn't.

PAUL. You can have it if you want it.

JOANNE. I'd have eaten it if I wanted it. I saved it for you.
Sharing it. Sharing it with you.

PAUL. Don't have to do that.

JOANNE. When was the last time you had a banana?

PAUL. Dunno. Couple of months.

JOANNE. There you go then. Team. You find a banana you
share it with me.

PAUL. Deal.

> PAUL *takes the banana and eats it*. JOANNE *watches
> every bite*.

> Tastes good.

JOANNE. Yeah.

PAUL. Thank you.

JOANNE. Anytime.

They smile at each other. They hug and hold onto each other. The hissing sound of the static from a tape player can be heard.

DAD (*on tape*). I catch food, I sell food, I cook food. There's pride in it, y'know?

YOUNG PAUL (*on tape*). Yeah.

...

Four days later.

JOANNE. You okay?

PAUL. Yeah. Tired. Just tired.

JOANNE. Always tired.

PAUL. Yeah.

JOANNE. Just you wait till you get that garlic under your eyelids, that'll wake you up.

PAUL. Can't wait.

JOANNE. See if you can swipe some bread.

PAUL. On my first shift?

JOANNE. No. Maybe not. Come on then, get going. Make a good impression and all that.

PAUL struggles a smile.

PAUL. Yeah. See you later.

PAUL exits. JOANNE watches him go. Without a distraction JOANNE is struck by hunger. She bites her nails. She scratches her head too hard. She paces. She stands but is never still. There is a stress building that she hasn't felt before.

...

Six days later. JOANNE *and* PAUL *stand.* JOANNE *is holding a payslip.*

PAUL. How much?

JOANNE. Less than last month. Not as many shifts for me now.

PAUL. Is it enough though?

JOANNE. Enough for rent and a bit of grub yeah. Enough for a holiday in Benidorm? Probably not. You been paid?

PAUL. No.

JOANNE. Right.

PAUL. Started at the end of the month, didn't I?

JOANNE. Right.

PAUL. You still overdrawn though?

JOANNE. Yeah, I will be.

PAUL. Okay.

JOANNE. Tough for us, isn't it?

    JOANNE *fidgets.*

PAUL. When the going gets tough, the tough get going, right? We're earning. We get paid. That's better than some. Just need to make it stretch. Tins and stuff. Tins are cheap.

JOANNE. Might go to bed for a bit.

PAUL. Okay.

    Beat.

JOANNE. You eaten today?

PAUL. Yeah.

JOANNE. What?

PAUL. Rice. Rice and ketchup. Some other bits.

JOANNE. How was it?

PAUL. Not going to put it in my cookbook. It was okay. You?

JOANNE. Garlic bread.

PAUL. Nick it?

JOANNE. –

PAUL. Can't keep nicking. If you lose your job –

JOANNE. You'll have to earn it all.

Beat.

I won't. It was a one-time thing. Promise.

PAUL. Regent will open again soon.

JOANNE. No it won't.

PAUL. Definitely will. You just wait.

JOANNE. Going to bed for a bit.

JOANNE *leaves the space.* PAUL *stands as the hissing static from the tape fills his memory. It's clear that Dad has been drinking.*

YOUNG PAUL (*on tape*). Tell me a story, Dad.

DAD (*on tape*). No.

YOUNG PAUL (*on tape*). Tell me a funny story.

DAD (*on tape*). No funny stories left. All rain and shadow and sad stories around here, Paul. That's all. Just sad stories.

YOUNG PAUL (*on tape*). Don't want a sad story.

DAD (*on tape*). Rain and shadow and nothing else. You got to dream big, Paul. You've got to dream so big. Do you think you can do that? Promise me you'll do that.

YOUNG PAUL (*on tape*). I promise.

DAD (*on tape*). Good boy.

...

Several days later PAUL *is curled up on the sofa.* JOANNE *stands but is not still.*

JOANNE. Hungry now.

PAUL. Yeah.

JOANNE. Properly hungry now.

PAUL. You okay?

JOANNE. Yeah. Yeah.

> *The energy soon leaves her. She sits. She looks at* PAUL. PAUL *can't meet her eye.*
>
> I feel sick. Mouth feels like it's had sick in it. Starving but I feel really sick.

PAUL. It passes.

JOANNE. Good.

PAUL. Get paid soon. We'll be alright when we get paid.

JOANNE. Yeah. Soon. Starving now though.

PAUL. Yeah.

> *Beat.*

JOANNE. Went to the supermarket today.

PAUL. Did you?

JOANNE. Yeah.

PAUL. Why?

JOANNE. To look.

PAUL. Nicking?

JOANNE. No! Just wanted to look. There was so much. So much food. Never noticed before just how much food there is in ASDA. Literally tonnes of food. Fucking shelves are bending from the weight of it all. Food in shiny, colourful packets. Every colour. Every flavour. Everything. Not for us though.

PAUL. Get paid soon. I've done nights. We'll be fine when we
    get paid.

JOANNE. Yeah.

PAUL. You okay?

JOANNE. Yeah.

...

Two days later. JOANNE *enters with a plastic bag. She takes
out half a sandwich and places it on the table. She cuts it in
half. She wants to share it with* PAUL. *She wants to eat it all
herself.*

JOANNE. Paul!

> *She eats her half. It tastes amazing. She can taste every
> single ingredient. She swallows. It hits her stomach hard.
> Immediately it hurts her. She cramps and curls up in pain.
> She retches. Slowly the cramps and retching passes. She
> stands and holds her stomach like it's broken.*

Paul!

> *He doesn't respond. She looks at the sandwich.*

Paul.

> *He doesn't respond. She eats his half. The cramp happens
> again, worse this time. It takes her to her knees, but she still
> eats the sandwich. She finishes it but can't move from the
> ground.*

> PAUL *enters. He cradles her.* JOANNE *is crying.*

I ate it all. Someone left a sandwich on the table at work and
    I ate it all. I was so hungry, Paul.

PAUL. That's okay.

JOANNE. I'm sorry.

PAUL. It's okay. It's okay. Get paid soon. Everything is okay.
    Do you want to hear a story?

JOANNE. No.

PAUL. It's funny. It's a really funny story. It'll make you laugh.

JOANNE. No thanks.

...

The next day. JOANNE enters, she is carrying a large box of food. She places it on a table and looks at it. She looks at it for a long time. A feeling grows. She can't breathe properly. Slowly she walks over to the box and takes out a packet of pasta. She looks at it.

PAUL *enters.*

PAUL. Alright?

JOANNE. Alright?

PAUL. What's going on?

JOANNE. Nothing much.

PAUL. What's that?

JOANNE. Got some grub.

PAUL. Where did you get it?

JOANNE. Never you mind, nosey beak.

PAUL. You been paid early?

JOANNE. No.

PAUL. I don't understand.

JOANNE. Nothing to understand. We didn't have food and now we do. Better get cooking. What you gonna make us?

PAUL. You nick it?

JOANNE. What?! No!! Cheeky bastard. Look at it all. How am I going to nick all that? I'd need a van. Besides, I don't nick stuff, mate. I did it once. Need to provide. Can't nick every day. Sustainability innit?

PAUL. Where then?

JOANNE. Who cares? Get cooking. Whadya want? We got beans, want some beans? Got pasta. Look at all that beautiful twisty pasta.

PAUL. Where did you get it?

JOANNE. Fuck off asking, Paul, and just cook, will ya?

PAUL. Toothpaste.

JOANNE. Yeah, I know. Gonna get straight on that, I am.

PAUL. Chocolate.

    PAUL *takes the chocolate and unwraps it. He smells it.*

JOANNE. You like that?

PAUL. Yeah.

JOANNE. Good.

PAUL. Want some?

JOANNE. No.

PAUL. What, why not?

JOANNE. Just don't.

PAUL. What's wrong?

JOANNE. Nothing. Just don't want chocolate right now. Bit rich.

PAUL. Why you not eating it?

JOANNE. Brushing my teeth. Don't want chocolate, want to clean my mouth, mate. That okay with you?

PAUL. Where did you get the grub, Joanne?

JOANNE. Nowhere.

PAUL. Nowhere?

JOANNE. That's right. Can I brush my teeth now?

PAUL. You magic?

JOANNE. What? No.

PAUL. But you got grub from nowhere, must be magic.

JOANNE. Don't worry about it.

PAUL. Who lent you cash?

JOANNE. No one.

PAUL. Tell us.

JOANNE. Forget it. Just cook.

PAUL. I will. Just need to know. Who? Not my mum.

JOANNE. Just cook, mate.

PAUL. You didn't go – Jesus, did you go up to see my mum? Joanne!! Fuck's sake. I told you not to.

JOANNE. No. I don't even –

PAUL. I TOLD YOU NOT TO!

JOANNE. I didn't go anywhere near your fucking mum. I don't even know where she lives. I wouldn't know her if she came up to me.

PAUL. Where then? Where? Where did you get all of this food from? What did you do?

JOANNE. Didn't do anything. What does that mean, 'what did you do?'

PAUL. Where then?

JOANNE. Nowhere.

PAUL. Stop saying nowhere. You obviously got it from somewhere.

JOANNE. Fuck's sake, Paul. Have the chocolate, enjoy it and leave off asking me stuff.

PAUL. No. Where?

JOANNE. Nowhere.

PAUL. Where?

JOANNE. Nowhere.

PAUL. Where did you get it, Joanne? Where did you get the food? Where? Where? Answer the fucking question, Joanne and tell me where you got the food from.

JOANNE. Nowhere. Nowhere. I just got it. I just got it. I just got it. I JUST GOT IT.

JOANNE. Foodbank. Foodbank. Fuck me. If you're so desperate to know. I got it from the foodbank. It's cool.

PAUL. –

JOANNE. You can eat the chocolate now.

PAUL. No.

JOANNE. I knew you'd be like this. Eat the fucking chocolate.

PAUL. We've got to take it back.

JOANNE. What? No chance. Why?

PAUL. It's for fuckers that need it. People with nothing.

JOANNE. Are you serious? That's us, Paul.

PAUL. No it's not. Take it back.

JOANNE. We are poor fuckers with nothing. That is us. Haven't eaten properly for days. Haven't even brushed our teeth.

PAUL. We wouldn't be poor if you didn't drink all your wages. Take it back.

JOANNE. One night. I went out one night, a thousand years ago. I'm not on the smash every night. Oh, and fuck you, I earn it. I get the grub. Hunter gatherer over here, what are you doing other than moaning at the walls?

PAUL. I'm working there, aren't I? Nightshifts of garlic bread. We need to wait and get paid. We need to send it back and wait.

JOANNE. No fucking way.

PAUL *starts to gather up the food and put it into bags.*

PAUL. We catch food, we sell food, we cook food, we don't take food for free. It's about pride.

JOANNE. Leave it. Don't touch it. It's ours. It's for us. They gave it to us.

PAUL *pushes her away and bags up more food.*

JOANNE. It's ours, you prick. I carried that. I carried that box by myself.

PAUL. We don't need it.

JOANNE. We do. We do.

PAUL. I don't want it!!

JOANNE. Stop it.

PAUL. I DON'T WANT THIS FOOD!!! IT ISN'T FOR US!!!

JOANNE. It is. It is for us. They did an assessment. THEY DID AN ASSESSMENT!!

Beat.

PAUL. Talking about?

JOANNE. You don't just walk in and help yourself. They do an assessment. We were approved. It is for us. Too proud, Paul. It'll kill you that will. Or me. It'll kill one of us.

PAUL. Sort of assessment?

JOANNE. One where they work out whether you need a box of food or not. It's not heavy. Just a load of questions.

PAUL. Like?

JOANNE. Like, are you hungry? YES. When did you last eat? DUNNO. You should get yourself out the house and do it yourself, then you'd know.

PAUL. And they said that we are up for a foodbank just because you're hungry?

JOANNE. Because we haven't eaten properly for days. Yes.

PAUL. Lying, I can tell.

JOANNE. Just cook us some pasta, Paul. Do what you're good at.

PAUL. No.

JOANNE. Don't then. Do nothing. Do nothing and cry about it. I'll cook it. I'll do it all. I'll do it all!! I went up there and I got it. I walked into that place, and I took the tiny amount of pride that I have left, and I shoved it in the bin, and I got us what we needed. So don't you fucking dare take that back. Don't you fucking dare make that worthless.

PAUL. Just need to wait for our wages. It's not for people like us.

JOANNE. They're all like us, you proud fucker. They're all like us. They're all working. Fucking teacher up there, took her badge off and hid it in her pocket but I saw it. 'Teacher', it said on it. Fucking woman in nurse's uniform. All hanging their heads, just like I did. All looking at the fucking floor. All breathing really fucking hard. All wiping their eyes. All women. All women, with blokes too proud to bother, I'd say.

PAUL. Do they know about the flat?

JOANNE. What? No. What about it? No.

PAUL. Didn't have to give an address?

JOANNE. No. I can't remember. It's cool.

PAUL. Jesus.

JOANNE. They won't do anything.

PAUL. They'll check.

JOANNE. They won't, they're a charity, they won't check.

PAUL. They'll check. They'll definitely check.

JOANNE. They don't know it's you. I could be shacked up with your brother for all they know. Relax. They don't care about that. We need to eat, Paul. Said it yourself. We need grub. I got grub. It shook my soul to do it, but I did it. I did it. Don't see you doing fuck-all to help. Pissing me off, mate.

PAUL. Go then.

JOANNE. If you carry on like this, I might. It's not fun any more, Paul. You used to have a bit of hide on your back. These days it's just jelly. Get tough, Paul.

PAUL. Get tough!? Sort of help is that?

JOANNE. No help. It's just what we have to do. I've done the help and got us grub. You just need to get a bit tough and cook us some dinner.

PAUL. Jesus.

JOANNE. I need you to be tougher than this.

PAUL. I'm tired.

JOANNE. Tired. Always tired from doing nothing. You're gonna need to get some energy from somewhere.

PAUL. Am I?

JOANNE. Yeah. You have no idea, mate. You have no fucking clue.

PAUL. No clue about what?

JOANNE. Nothing.

PAUL. No clue about what? What does that mean, Joanne? WHAT DOES IT MEAN?!

JOANNE. It means I'm pregnant. There you go, prick, have that. That's why we got so much grub. That's why we passed the assessment. Are you hungry? YES. Are you without a means of providing food? YES. Are you pregnant? YES. No more questions after that one, just silence and pity and me trying really fucking hard not to break into a million pieces and then a big box with grub in it. And before you start crying, I'm keeping it. We are keeping it.

PAUL. –

JOANNE. So get tough and cook.

PAUL *looks at her for a long time. He thinks a million different thoughts all at the same time.*

PAUL. I want you to go now.

JOANNE. Go? The fuck does that mean?

PAUL. It means you can go. Get out. Take the food and go away.

JOANNE. What?

PAUL. Get out of my flat now please.

JOANNE. It's dark. It's night out there.

PAUL. Get out!

JOANNE. I think you need to stop speaking. Because one day this kid is going to ask us about this moment, and you do not want me to tell it that you kicked me out of the house when you found out you were going to be a dad. Is that what you want?!

PAUL. Too much pressure. Like a pressure cooker on full heat with no fucking fluid in there. That's how I feel. Every time you walk through the door, the heat goes up. The heat goes up. The heat just goes up!

JOANNE. Fine! Fine. I'll kip under the bridge with all the dead pigeons. I've done it before. It's not so bad. Better than this shithole anyway. Prick!

PAUL. –

JOANNE. –

PAUL. –

JOANNE. What?

PAUL. –

JOANNE. Nothing?

PAUL. –

JOANNE. Pregnant and sleeping under the bridge. That cool with you, is it?

PAUL. GET OUT!!

JOANNE. I'M GOING! Don't want to stay here anyway.

JOANNE *grabs a bag of food and leaves. As she hits the edge of the space she turns back.*

It's a girl by the way. They told me today. She's going to fucking hate you. Just so you know.

JOANNE *leaves the space.* PAUL *still can't find the fight.*

PAUL *stands still. As tension grows inside him, he starts to move a little bit.*

Time passes.

JOANNE *steps onto the boat. She sits and wraps a blanket around herself. She eats.*

PAUL *stands and remembers.*

Time passes.

On the boat, JOANNE *finds the tapes. In amongst them is a tape recorder. She puts a cassette into the recorder and presses play.*

The hissing static of the tape can be heard.

PAUL *stands consumed by memory.*

JOANNE *listens.*

YOUNG PAUL (*on tape*). Food's ready.

DAD (*on tape*). Pass me the drink.

YOUNG PAUL (*on tape*). Finished it.

DAD (*on tape*). There's another one somewhere.

YOUNG PAUL (*on tape*). Don't need another one, Dad.

DAD (*on tape*). Need or want. That's the question. Don't need much, can live on very little. But we want what we want.

YOUNG PAUL (*on tape*). Stop it, Dad.

DAD (*on tape*). Don't stop me, Paul. Don't do that, son.

YOUNG PAUL (*on tape*). Thought you were working tonight. Thought you were going to catch some fish.

DAD (*on tape*). No point. Too late. Gonna eat pie with my boy.

YOUNG PAUL (*on tape*). Not hungry.

DAD (*on tape*). Yes you are.

YOUNG PAUL (*on tape*). Not.

DAD (*on tape*). I love you son.

YOUNG PAUL (*on tape*). Shut up, Dad.

DAD (*on tape*). I do.

YOUNG PAUL (*on tape*). Just drunk. Say it all the time it doesn't mean anything.

DAD (*on tape*). I do though. Eat with me. Sit and eat.

YOUNG PAUL (*on tape*). Not hungry.

DAD (*on tape*). Eat with me, Paul. Dying man's wish.

YOUNG PAUL (*on tape*). Drunk man's wish.

DAD (*on tape*). Taught you to cook.

YOUNG PAUL (*on tape*). I know. So?

DAD (*on tape*). Taught you so that you can be better. Better than me. Taught you so you don't have to fish. Taught you to cook and find good food, proper food, so you can be better, bigger and better. Like snakes and ladders around here, Paul. Like snakes and ladders without the ladders.

Eat with me.

YOUNG PAUL (*on tape*). No.

DAD (*on tape*). Caught in a net. Caught in a net and every way I turn it just gets tighter. You got to dream big, Paul. So, you don't get caught too. Do you think you can do that?

YOUNG PAUL (*on tape*). Don't know.

DAD (*on tape*). Got to try. Got to really try. Dream big. Bigger than I did. Got to push for something better. Promise me.

YOUNG PAUL (*on tape*). I'll try.

DAD (*on tape*). More than try. Promise.

YOUNG PAUL (*on tape*). I promise.

DAD (*on tape*). You've said it now.

YOUNG PAUL (*on tape*). I know.

DAD (*on tape*). Can't break a dying man's promise.

YOUNG PAUL (*on tape*). Stop saying that.

DAD (*on tape*). I love you, Paul. I do. I really do.

YOUNG PAUL (*on tape*). Same.

The hissing sound of the tape grows and grows and grows. The tape stops.

...

Two days later. JOANNE *sits on the boat. She is wrapped in an old blanket.*

PAUL *enters.*

PAUL. Alright?

JOANNE *can't meet his eye.*

Found you.

JOANNE. –

PAUL. Cold on here.

JOANNE. –

PAUL. You okay?

JOANNE. Go away, Paul.

PAUL. Cold on here. No diesel to warm it up.

JOANNE. Better than the streets.

PAUL. Yeah.

   Beat.

   You okay?

JOANNE. No. Fuck off.

PAUL. –

   JOANNE *eyeballs* PAUL.

JOANNE. That it?

PAUL. What?

JOANNE. You okay? That all you got?

PAUL. Sorry.

JOANNE. Not even close, mate.

PAUL. I don't know… I don't know what to say. Everything's gone to shit.

JOANNE. Not everything.

PAUL. No. Sorry.

JOANNE. What you doing here?

PAUL. I cooked you something.

JOANNE. I don't want it.

PAUL. Sausage casserole. Had to use baked beans instead of cannellini but –

JOANNE. Keep it.

PAUL. Must be starving.

JOANNE. Nope.

PAUL. It's nice. All foodbank.

JOANNE. Looks like shit. Looks cold.

PAUL. I've got gas.

JOANNE. That'll be the beans.

PAUL. Gas for the stove.

JOANNE. Where did you get gas from? You been earning for once?

PAUL. Mum's.

JOANNE. You nick it from her shed?

PAUL. No! I went to see her.

JOANNE. Right. Nice. Happy families.

Silence. Stillness.

PAUL. Sorry.

JOANNE. You said.

PAUL. Sorry.

JOANNE. Are ya?

PAUL. Yeah.

JOANNE. Not good enough.

PAUL. Just didn't know what to do. It's all got fucked. My head's a mess.

JOANNE. Kicked me out!

PAUL. Sorry.

JOANNE. Kicked me out because I am pregnant, Paul.

PAUL. Not because –

JOANNE. Really?

PAUL. Yeah.

JOANNE. Why then? Because it sounded like it.

PAUL. Because my head's a mess.

JOANNE. Tidy it up then because it's making you act like a dick.

PAUL. Not as easy as that.

JOANNE. Easy? Nothing's easy, Paul. Easy isn't here, mate. I've never known easy. What you gonna do, cry?

PAUL. I'm caught in a net.

JOANNE. I spend all my time trying to drag you up when all you want to do is sink. Not got the strength any more. You can fucking sink, you can drown in it now.

PAUL. –

JOANNE. Standing there, saying nothing. Go away.

PAUL. I don't want to.

JOANNE. Kicked me out, Paul.

PAUL. Sorry. It's… I didn't mean to.

JOANNE. No fight in ya.

PAUL. –

JOANNE. No fight in ya, Paul.

PAUL. No.

JOANNE. Scared.

PAUL. Probably.

JOANNE. You've got two choices. Be like me and fight, or don't fight and be like your dad.

   PAUL *looks at her. He notices the cassette.*

PAUL. Did you listen to it?

JOANNE. Yeah.

PAUL. You listened to my tapes?

JOANNE. Nowt else to do. No Netflix on here, boy.

PAUL. Shouldn't have done that.

JOANNE. Well I did.

PAUL. Not yours. Not your fucking property.

JOANNE. Shouldn't have kicked me out onto the street then, should you?

PAUL. Put it back.

JOANNE. Put it back yourself.

PAUL. Could have broken it!

JOANNE. So? Should have done. Better if I had done.

PAUL. Shut up.

JOANNE. Care more about your tapes than me. Care more about your dead dad than your own kid.

PAUL. You don't just listen to someone's private tapes. Who does that?

JOANNE. Me.

PAUL. Yeah. You!

JOANNE. I do what I want. And I wouldn't have listened to it if you hadn't kicked me OUT! Boring anyway. Just a kid crying about his pissed-up, washed-up mess of a dad!

PAUL. Shut up.

JOANNE. He sounded like a joke-man. Sounded like a fucking loser.

PAUL. Shut up.

JOANNE. Sounded like you. / Scared, like a baby. Like a baby!!

PAUL. STOP IT!

PAUL *screams*.

STOP IT!!!! STOP IT!!!

Rage is burning through him. It's physical and volatile and explosive.

JOANNE *laughs at him.*

JOANNE. Finally! A bit of fight. Not enough, but it's a start.

PAUL. Stressing me out. Can't breathe from it.

> PAUL *paces. Energy is pulsing through him. He stops and curls up into a ball. He tenses up further.* PAUL *uncurls and stands.*

JOANNE. You do.

PAUL. What?

JOANNE. Sound like him.

PAUL. Shut up.

JOANNE. Sound like him now. Made him drink. Makes you stand still.

> PAUL *looks at her. She looks back.*

> Makes you stop.

PAUL. Comes in waves. Like the sea. Tides. Goes away and comes back. Always going away or coming back. Relentless.

JOANNE. Gotta get that out, mate. It'll chew you up, make you go bad.

PAUL. I'm fine.

JOANNE. You're not.

PAUL. Comes in waves. It'll go again.

JOANNE. And then it'll come back.

> JOANNE *points to her stomach.*

> Gonna do the same to this one? Gonna fuck her up like he did to you? Gonna make her go bad?

PAUL. No.

JOANNE. Really? Cos it's a shit start.

PAUL. I'm here, aren't I? Made a casserole.

JOANNE. Wow. Casserole. Hero.

PAUL. I'm trying. Fighting. A bit.

JOANNE. Superhero. I might fall over in a minute from all your heroics.

PAUL. Let me breathe, Joanne. You never let me breathe.

JOANNE. Think you can smooth it over with sausage and beans.

PAUL. No.

JOANNE. Kicked me out. Have you any idea how many people have kicked me out in my life.

PAUL. I know. Sorry.

JOANNE. Like a baby, like the child on that tape stood in front of me.

PAUL. Sorry. I said sorry. I didn't mean to.

JOANNE. But you did.

PAUL. Got caught, that's all. Got caught up, couldn't breathe.

JOANNE. Stop talking like him. Stop saying his words, it's weird.

PAUL. Promised him. Promised him I'd do something. Be better.

JOANNE. So? Bin it.

PAUL. I was on it. I was halfway there.

JOANNE. Until you chipped into me.

PAUL. Until The Regent closed.

JOANNE. Other jobs out there, big man.

PAUL. Not good ones.

JOANNE. Fuck 'good'. Who cares about 'good'.

PAUL. We should go. Get out of here. Go somewhere better.

JOANNE. I'm fine where I am.

PAUL. Joking aren't ya?

JOANNE. What's wrong with it? You always want better, Paul. There is no better. Chasing smoke, mate.

PAUL. Got nowhere to live soon.

JOANNE. Got nowhere to live anywhere else. You look at it through your dad's drunken eyes, mate. That's all. That fucking promise will kill you, mate; it's weighing you down. Shut it out. It means nothing.

PAUL. Nothing left around here 'cept broken boats and dead dreams. That's all there is. Rain and shadow.

JOANNE. Saying his words, Paul. Stop it. It's no better anywhere else, mate. I've been climbing out of windows all my life. It doesn't make a difference.

PAUL. He knew that it was going to shit around here.

JOANNE. Shit everywhere if you just look at the shit.

PAUL. We should get out.

JOANNE. Stop talking like him.

PAUL. We should go.

JOANNE. Stop listening to him, Paul.

JOANNE *grabs a tape and pulls a little bit out.*

PAUL. STOP!! DON'T!!

JOANNE. Stop listening to him then.

PAUL. Put it down.

JOANNE *pulls a little bit more.*

I made a promise!!

JOANNE. You were eleven years old. He was pissed. Fuck him off. Let it all go, mate. It's messing with your head.

PAUL. Please can I have my tape back?

JOANNE *throws the tape on the floor.*

JOANNE. Like a baby. You're exhausting, you know that? Don't actually know why I'm bothering, to be honest.

PAUL. I was halfway there.

JOANNE. Halfway where? You're not making sense.

PAUL. Career. Cookbook. Safety. Stuff like that. I'm not even cooking any more.

JOANNE. You are. Fucking casserole over there.

PAUL. That's shit.

JOANNE. Lovely. I was actually looking forward to that.

PAUL. It's tins from a foodbank.

JOANNE. And? What is wrong with that? You made a casserole with it. Who does that? Do you know what most people would cook with sausage and beans? Sausage and beans and most people would fuck that up. I would. But you wouldn't. You made a casserole and apologised for using baked beans instead of posh ones.

PAUL. Cannellini.

JOANNE. Whatever. I've literally no idea what that is. Something different about you. Lots different about you, actually but let's just focus on the cooking. Your dad taught you to cook. Cook. Cook with what you've got.

PAUL. Got nowhere to live.

JOANNE. Got a boat. Live on here.

PAUL. Freezing, Joanne.

JOANNE. Get a heater!! Stop blocking me. Don't need to pay rent if you live on here. Do what you're good at. You used to bang on about being good.

PAUL. I am good.

JOANNE. Be good then. Good at doing nothing at the minute. Prove that you're good. Did it to me. Prove to your daughter that you're not a waste of space.

PAUL. I don't know how to.

JOANNE. Holy shit. I'm going to stop in a minute. Just so you
know, I am going to stop fighting for you in a minute and
I'm going to walk away. You keep blocking me and I will
walk away. This is my last go. I hope your ears are switched
on because I fucking *promise* you, I mean it, I will leave. Are
you listening?

PAUL. Yeah.

JOANNE. You are good at cooking. Very good at cooking.
Better than anyone I know. It's a skill, a talent, whatever. So,
use it. Get grub from foodbank because that's all we've got
right now. Cook it for me and your daughter that's in my
belly. Get another cooking job. Get serious at looking for a
job and you will find one. It might not be fine dining to posh
folk, but it will be good food for good people. Save some
wedge. Keep cooking, keep proving to people that you're
good, don't stop, don't ever stop. Live happily ever after.
The end.

JOANNE *flops down, exhausted.*

Knackered now.

PAUL. Bit cheesy.

JOANNE. Yeah well you weren't bloody listening to anything
else.

PAUL. Good food for good people. Reckon we can do it?

JOANNE. Can do anything. Can do anything at all. Cos if you
don't, you may as well just dig a hole and sit in it. In
eighteen years, your daughter comes to you and says life's
shit, no jobs, the world's a mess, no hope anywhere. But
she's mega good at... I don't know... singing. She's
unbelievable at it, when she sings it makes you cry with joy,
makes you laugh, makes you shiver. What do you say to her?

PAUL. Be a singer. Don't let nobody stop you.

JOANNE. Correct. Now get that gas on and cook the sausages, I'm done in now.

JOANNE *lies down*. PAUL *sits still*.

Thinking about it?

PAUL. Yeah, I am. Good food for good people.

JOANNE. Not a bad name for a cookbook, that.

PAUL *smiles*.

You wanna chuck those tapes in the sea too? Strike while the iron's hot.

PAUL. Don't think so.

JOANNE. I mean it.

PAUL. I can't.

JOANNE. Can't. Can. Choose who you listen to.

PAUL. It makes me remember him.

JOANNE. I know. Chuck them in the sea, you'll hear him clearer. Better. You'll remember more. I promise you will.

PAUL. Can't.

JOANNE. Then you just need a woman who can. Don't worry about it, I'll do it when you're asleep.

PAUL *thinks*.

Gradually PAUL *starts to move. Almost automatically, as if he is regaining feeling in his limbs, he cooks.*

...

Three months later. JOANNE *is pregnant and showing. They are still on the boat. There is a small heater and few other bits of comfort – a lamp and maybe a cushion.* PAUL *has cooked.*

JOANNE. What have we got?

PAUL. Fish pie.

JOANNE. Nice.

PAUL. Used to cook it with him. Feels right. I put boiled egg in it though, so.

JOANNE. Smooth.

Beat.

You ready, then?

PAUL. No. Yeah.

JOANNE *hands* PAUL *a pair of scissors.* PAUL *takes the scissors.* JOANNE *hands him a cassette tape.* PAUL *looks at it.*

JOANNE. You'll hear him clearer. I promise you will.

PAUL. It's his voice though.

JOANNE. You don't need to listen to it, not to remember him. He's in everything you cook. He's in the taste and smell and the joy that people feel when they eat your food. He's in their smiles, not on that tape. That's not him. That's the broken version. Let him go.

PAUL *looks at the cassette. Eventually and very slowly he pulls a tiny bit of the tape. He stops. He pulls a little bit more. He pulls and pulls and pulls.*

PAUL *cuts the tape. His dad's voice fills his memory.* PAUL *can hear him clearly, there is no static.*

DAD. I love you, Paul.

YOUNG PAUL. Dad!

DAD. Eat with me, son.

They eat.

Taste good?

YOUNG PAUL. Tastes amazing.

DAD. I love you. I really do.

YOUNG PAUL. Same.

JOANNE. Well done. How do you feel?

PAUL. Good. Sad.

JOANNE. Let's eat.

There is no food, they don't mime but we know they have eaten.

PAUL. How is it?

JOANNE. Good with the egg. Doesn't it make it taste better?

PAUL. No.

JOANNE. Yes it does.

PAUL. I made pudding too.

JOANNE. I haven't had this yet. What is it then? I can tell you want to show it to me.

PAUL produces a bowl of butterscotch Angel Delight.

PAUL. Butterscotch flavour.

JOANNE. You soppy fucker.

PAUL. Family food.

JOANNE takes a spoon and fills it with Angel Delight. She eats.

JOANNE. Incredible. That is the best thing you have ever cooked.

She offers him a spoonful.

Want some?

PAUL. No, ta.

JOANNE. Eat it.

PAUL. I'm alright.

JOANNE. Family food. You want to be a family; you'll eat the Delight. Eat it! Eat the Delight.

PAUL eats it. It tastes disgusting.

Too posh, mate. It's amazing.

PAUL. I love you.

JOANNE. Easy. It's only Angel Delight.

PAUL. I do.

JOANNE. Right. Okay. Well, yeah... same.

Blackout.

www.nickhernbooks.co.uk

facebook.com/nickhernbooks

twitter.com/nickhernbooks